NOTEBOOK

ISBN 979-8-89686-514-8

NOTEBOOK

Peter McIntosh

Contents

Prologue

The golden hues of late afternoon stretched lazily across the sky as the five teenagers sprawled out on the worn wooden dock, their laughter echoing over the still water. The lake had been their refuge for as long as they could remember—a place untouched by the weight of expectations, where time seemed to slow just for them.

Ellie lay on her stomach, sketchpad balanced on the edge of the dock, capturing the scene before her in quick, confident strokes. The quiet lapping of the water against the posts mixed with the distant rustling of leaves, soothing and familiar.

Zara sat cross-legged, flipping a worn soccer ball between her hands, her eyes scanning the horizon like she was searching for something—perhaps an answer, perhaps just peace. Even here, Zara's mind worked, organising, strategizing, though for once, there was nothing that needed fixing.

Max adjusted his glasses, staring at his phone screen as Baxter, his golden retriever, sat attentively beside him, panting happily. Max swore he was just checking the weather, but the others knew better. He always had an eye on the real world, cautious and sceptical, ever the realist in a group full of dreamers and daredevils.

Theo leaned back on his elbows, staring at the sky as Shadow, his greyhound, dozed at his feet. His usual sharp remarks were absent, replaced by a rare moment of stillness. There was something about this place that softened even the hardest edges, though Theo would never admit it.

And then there was Jake—dangling precariously from a tree branch just above the water, grinning like he had already won some unspoken challenge. "Bet I can do a backflip into the lake without even making a splash," he announced.

"Bet you can't," Zara countered, smirking as she spun the soccer ball on her fingertip.

Jake waggled his eyebrows. "That sounds like a challenge."

"It is," Theo added flatly, not bothering to look up.

Jake didn't hesitate. He leaped, twisting in the air—

And landed with the most spectacular belly flop imaginable.

Laughter erupted from the dock as Jake surfaced, sputtering and grinning. "Okay, maybe a small splash."

Ellie chuckled, shaking her head as she sketched the moment in the corner of her page. This was what mattered. Not the worries of school, not the expectations waiting for them beyond the lake, but right here, right now—warm sunlight, lazy afternoons.

The next day, morning sun spilled golden light over the quiet town, seeping through Ellie's curtains and warming her face. Luna, curled at the foot of her bed, stretched lazily before hopping down with a soft thud. Ellie blinked awake, the scent of fresh coffee drifting up from the kitchen.

It was the kind of morning that promised another day of easy laughter and unspoken adventure.

8

By midday, the five of them had gathered at Zara's house, sprawled across her backyard. Max sat cross-legged in the shade, tinkering with some gadget he had pulled apart. Baxter, his golden retriever, flopped next to him, panting happily.

"You're going to break that," Theo muttered, tossing a small ball for Shadow, his greyhound, who barely hesitated before sprinting after it.

Max scoffed, adjusting his glasses. "I'm improving it."

Jake, lying on his back in the grass, hands behind his head, grinned. "Famous last words, buddy." Milo, his ferret, darted across the grass, attempting to steal a chip from Jake's bag.

Zara stood, stretching. "Alright, we're not wasting another perfect day sitting here."

Ellie smirked, sketchpad resting on her lap. "Didn't you say that yesterday?"

"And look how much fun we had," Zara shot back. "Now, are we going to the lake or what?"

The answer was obvious.

9

Within an hour, they were there, the water shimmering under the sun. Theo had claimed the old wooden dock, dipping his feet into the cool water while pretending not to enjoy himself. Zara was already diving in, her laughter ringing across the lake. Max, after much hesitation, waded in up to his knees, muttering about the unknown creatures lurking beneath the surface.

Jake, meanwhile, was attempting to stand on a makeshift raft of logs and rope, arms flailing dramatically. "I am the captain of this fine—" The raft wobbled. "—impressive vessel, and I command—" The logs shifted and with a mighty splash, he was in the water, resurfacing with a triumphant grin. "Totally meant to do that."

Ellie sat at the edge of the dock, feet swinging above the water, her pencil dancing across the page. She captured it all—the sun glinting off the ripples, Zara's confident strokes, Theo's contemplative stare, Max's careful steps, Jake's chaotic energy.

For now, everything was simple. No worries, no pressure. Just summer days, cool water, and the unbreakable rhythm of their friendship.

And they wanted to keep it that way, for as long as they could but the holidays were almost over.

Ellie sat on her bed that night, sketchpad resting on her knees, Luna curled beside her. She tried to capture the way the sunlight danced on the lake, the way Zara's hair clung to her face after swimming, the way Jake's grin never wavered, even when his so-called 'brilliant ideas' landed him in disaster.

She didn't want to forget any of it.

The others felt it too, even if they wouldn't say it out loud. Max, for one, had started muttering about unfinished projects, about school schedules and routines. "We should have started a week ago," he grumbled, adjusting his glasses as he worked on some half-built contraption in Zara's backyard. Baxter wagged his tail as if to say, *Relax, buddy.*

Theo shrugged it off, lying in the grass, arms behind his head.

"Plenty of time left," he said, but he wasn't fooling anyone.

Even he had stopped arguing whenever Zara suggested doing something fun.

So, they made the most of it.

One last late-night adventure, sneaking onto the roof of Max's garage to watch the stars. One last trip to the arcade, where Jake somehow convinced an entire group of kids that he was a pinball master (he wasn't). One last swim at the lake, where they stayed long past sunset, water glowing silver under the moonlight.

Zara splashed water at Ellie, grinning. "You're getting sentimental."

Ellie smirked. "And you're not?"

Zara hesitated, then shrugged. "Maybe a little."

Jake floated on his back, hands behind his head. "Don't get all dramatic, guys. We've still got a few days left."

But even he knew—their carefree summer was slipping through their fingers, like water through cupped hands. Soon, there would be early mornings and textbooks, deadlines and responsibilities.

Morning arrived slow and golden, the kind of quiet that felt like the world was holding its breath. It was their last day before alarm clocks replaced late mornings, before classrooms replaced open fields, before routine replaced freedom.
None of them said it out loud, but they all knew.
By noon, they had gathered at the lake one last time, as if staying there long enough would stretch the holiday time just a little further. Ellie sat on the dock, sketchpad open but untouched. She didn't want to draw today—she just wanted to remember.
Zara kicked at the water from where she sat next to her, eyes narrowed against the sun. "We should do something."

"We *are* doing something," Theo pointed out from the shade, tossing a stick for Shadow, who bolted after it.

Jake flopped onto the dock dramatically. "Theo, my man, this is *not* something. We need to make this day count."

Max, lying on his back in the grass, sighed. "Please tell me this doesn't involve anything dangerous."

Jake shot finger guns at him. "Danger is subjective, my friend."

Ellie smiled, shaking her head. "Alright, what's the plan?"

What followed was a chaotic blur of everything they could cram into one last day.

There was something about days like this—days that felt endless, even though deep down, they knew they weren't. The wind rushed past as they raced their bikes down the empty backroads, the sun warm against their skin, the air thick with the scent of sunbaked earth and wildflowers. Jake stood on his pedals, arms stretched out like he could take flight, laughing into the wind. "No hands, losers!"

Max scoffed. "You're *going* to crash."

Theo, riding beside him, smirked. "Yeah, and we're all supposed to act surprised when it happens?"

Zara, a few paces ahead, glanced back. "If he wipes out, I am *not* carrying him home."

Ellie just smiled, letting the moment sink into her bones. The way the world blurred past them, the laughter echoing in the air, the simple joy of moving fast with nowhere to be.

They raced their bikes through winding backroads, Zara leading the charge. They raided the corner store for snacks, pooling their spare change for way too many bags of crisps. They set up an impromptu picnic at their usual spot, Jake balancing on a fallen log as he delivered one of his infamous, nonsense-filled speeches about "the importance of living in the moment."

They sprawled out in the grass, their stomachs full of snacks from the corner store. The sky stretched wide and endless

15

above them, clouds shifting lazily, the water shimmering in the golden afternoon light.

Ellie traced patterns in the air with her fingers, imagining the shapes becoming sketches on a blank page. "That one looks like a dragon," she murmured, pointing at a drifting cloud.

Zara squinted. "No way. That's obviously a horse."

"You're both wrong," Jake declared, waving his arms dramatically. "That's a cosmic space chicken."

Theo groaned. "You're unbearable."

A comfortable silence settled over them, the kind that only happens when there's nowhere else to be, nothing else to do but *exist*.

Ellie wished she could bottle this feeling, capture it in a sketch or a snapshot—something to hold onto when life became busy again.

But maybe that was the point. Maybe some moments weren't meant to be kept. Maybe they were meant to be felt, fully and completely, before letting them drift away like clouds in a summer sky.

So, she didn't try to hold onto it.

She just breathed it in.

The sun sank lower.

Evening found them at the lake, sitting on the dock, feet dangling over the edge. The sky burned orange and pink, the water reflecting its colours like melted gold.

"I wish we had more time," Ellie murmured, hugging her knees to her chest.

Zara nudged her shoulder. "We'll still have weekends."

"And after-school" Jake added.

"Sure," Theo smirked. "If Max can survive his workload."

Max huffed. "I hate that you're not wrong."

Silence stretched between them, comfortable but heavy.

Eventually, Jake stood, stretching. "Alright, one last swim before summer officially dies. Who's in?"

Without hesitation, Zara dove in after him, sending a splash across the dock. Theo, with a sigh like he couldn't believe he was doing this, followed. Max hesitated, but Ellie took his hand and pulled him along.

The water was cold but freeing, and for a few more moments, summer was still theirs.

Tomorrow, everything would go back to normal.

But tonight, they were *here*. And that was enough.

Ellie stared at her alarm clock, blinking against the harsh red numbers flashing **6:30 AM**. It buzzed again, and Luna, curled at the foot of her bed, stretched before flicking her tail in mild annoyance.

It was officially over.

With a sigh, Ellie pushed herself out of bed, her limbs heavy from the weight of schedules, expectations, and the thought of hallways packed with students. No more lazy afternoons by the lake, no more racing down backroads, no more endless nights under the stars.

The five of them met up outside the school gates, like they always did. But something about it felt different now, like the world had shifted overnight.

Zara was already in full focus mode, clutching a neatly organised binder. "Alright, guys. We survived the break. Now, we get back to work."

Jake groaned, slinging an arm over her shoulder. "*Ugh,* don't say it like that. You make it sound like a prison sentence."

Theo, leaning against the fence, smirked. "Because it kind of is."

Max, adjusting his glasses, muttered, "Not helping, Theo."

Ellie stayed quiet, just *watching* them—how the energy felt different, how the weight of schedules and assignments already loomed over them.

But then Jake grinned and clapped his hands together.

"Alright, listen up, people. New year, same us. No way we're letting school kill our vibes."

Zara rolled her eyes. "And how exactly do you plan on stopping it?"

Jake grinned wider. "We *live in the moment,* remember?"

Ellie smiled at that. Maybe summer was over. Maybe routine had taken its place.

But Jake was right. *They* were still here. And that meant they could still find ways to make the ordinary feel a little *extraordinary.*

Maybe the fun wasn't over. Maybe it was just changing.

And maybe that wasn't such a bad thing.

The first week back always brought the same routine— syllabuses handed out, lockers slammed shut, teachers going on about "a fresh start." But for Ellie and the others, it wasn't just about getting back into the rhythm of school.

It was about figuring out what came next.

They gathered at their usual lunch table, trays pushed aside as Zara pulled out a notebook. "Alright," she said, flipping to a fresh page. "Let's talk goals."

Jake groaned. "*Ugh*, can't we just live in the moment?"

"We *are* in the moment," Zara shot back. "But even 'moment people' need direction."

Theo smirked. "She's not wrong, for once."

Ellie listened, twirling a pencil between her fingers. The idea of *goals* always felt... heavy. Like making them meant she could also *fail* them.

But maybe that was the point.

Zara tapped her pen against the table. "Alright, I'll start. I want to make the soccer team again *and* get through tutoring without losing my mind."

Max adjusted his glasses. "I want to actually *survive* my classes without burning out."

Theo leaned back. "I don't know, not failing sounds like a solid goal."

Jake grinned. "My goal is to *make this year fun.*"

Zara narrowed her eyes. "That's not a real goal."

"It *totally* is."

Ellie hesitated when they turned to her. She had goals—sort of. Get better at her art. Maybe enter a contest. Maybe even show people her work instead of hiding it.

But saying it out loud made it *real.*

"I... want to push myself more," she finally said. "With my art. Maybe do something with it instead of just keeping it to myself."

Zara gave a satisfied nod. "Now *that's* a goal."

They went around, adding more—some big, some small, some half-joking (Jake swore he was going to teach Milo, his ferret, to do tricks). But by the time the bell rang, something had shifted.

They weren't just *going* through the year. They were *building* it.

22

Maybe the days of freedom were behind them. But that didn't mean the days ahead had to be *boring*.

And maybe, just maybe, their goals would shape something even better than they expected.

Ellie trudged into the kitchen, rubbing sleep from her eyes as Luna wound around her ankles. The smell of coffee drifted from the pot, but it wasn't enough to shake off the weight of routine settling back onto her shoulders.

By the time she met the others at school, the general mood was *exhausted*.

Jake slumped over the lunch table. "We've been back *three days*, and I'm already done."

Max, who looked slightly more awake, pushed his glasses up his nose. "Maybe if you went to bed before *2 AM*, you wouldn't feel like a zombie."

Jake waved a hand dismissively. "Details."

Zara sighed, flipping open her planner. "Okay, *this* is exactly why we need good daily habits."

Theo raised an eyebrow. "Here we go."

"No, really," Zara insisted. "We can't just wing it every day. We have classes, practices, homework—"

"*Fun*," Jake added.

"—*and* fun," she allowed, "but if we don't manage our time, we're all going to crash and burn before we get to the half term break."

Ellie tapped her pencil against the table. "She's not wrong."

Max nodded. "Building good habits now makes everything easier later."

Theo smirked. "Like what? Sleep? Food? Actually doing homework on time?"

"Yes," Zara said. "All of that."

They went around the table, suggesting habits they *knew* would make a difference:

- **Ellie:** Drawing every day, even for just five minutes, so she didn't lose her creativity in the chaos of school.

- **Zara:** Keeping a schedule to balance soccer, tutoring, and schoolwork.
- **Max:** Actually getting *enough* sleep instead of pulling late-night study sessions.
- **Theo:** Eating *real* food instead of just energy drinks and snacks.
- **Jake:** ...Trying to wake up on time. Maybe. No promises.

By the end of lunch, it wasn't just about school—it was about *making life easier.*

Jake stretched. "Alright, alright, I'll admit it—maybe routines aren't *all* bad."

Zara smirked. "Told you."

Max grinned. "We'll check back in a week and see how we're doing."

Ellie leaned back, feeling something settle into place. The holidays had been about freedom. But maybe the school year didn't have to be a drag—maybe with the right habits, they could make it *work for them.*

Chapter 1 - The gift

Ellie didn't believe in magic. At least, not the kind that filled the pages of her favourite fantasy novels, or the kind her younger brother, Daniel, liked to tell stories about. Magic was just a thing of imagination, of escape, and for Ellie, who was more comfortable with a pencil in her hand than anything else, it was just another element of the world she could control with her art.

But as she stood in the dust-dappled loft of her grandmother's old house, one foot on a wobbly chair, the other firmly planted on the creaky floorboards, Ellie was about to find out that not all magic could be drawn.

She wiped a stray strand of auburn hair from her face and squinted at the box in front of her. It was small, plain, covered in faded, peeling brown paper. Nothing extraordinary about it. But something about it called to her, nestled in the corner of the loft, half-buried beneath old books and forgotten knick-knacks.

"Ellie! What are you doing up there?" Daniel's voice echoed up from the hallway, breaking her concentration. She sighed, rolling her eyes.

"Just looking for something to draw in, Dan! Chill out!" Ellie called back, although she wasn't entirely sure what she was searching for. A sketchbook, maybe? Her old one had disappeared ages ago, and she hadn't bothered replacing it. The loft was quiet now that her grandmother's house was empty, but Ellie had always loved the space. The smell of dust and old wood, the quiet solitude—it was the perfect place for thinking and drawing.

Ellie reached down and lifted the box carefully. The lid creaked open with a resistance that made her fingers tingle with anticipation. She paused, letting the air settle before peering inside. It was filled with layers of yellowed parchment, tied with fraying string. Beneath the papers, something

metallic glinted in the dim light. A small notebook.

Ellie's heart skipped a beat. The notebook was old, its leather

cover worn and soft to the touch. The pages inside were

empty—at least, at first glance. She flipped through them

quickly, but every page was blank, devoid of any marks or

scribbles. Except, there was something peculiar about the last

page. A strange, ornate symbol was etched in the corner, a

swirl of lines that seemed to shimmer faintly beneath her

fingers.

"Ellie, what's taking so long?" Daniel's voice drifted up again.

This notebook was calling to her in a way she couldn't explain.

She quickly tucked it under her arm and jumped down from

the chair, landing lightly on the floor.

"Just found something," she mumbled, heading toward the

stairs, the notebook clutched in her hands.

That night, Ellie sat at her desk, the notebook open in front of her. The room was quiet, lit only by the soft glow of a single lamp on the desk. Outside, the wind rustled the trees, but inside, there was a stillness that made Ellie feel as though the whole world was holding its breath.

She had to admit, there was something about the notebook that intrigued her. It wasn't like any sketchbook she'd ever owned. It felt different, almost alive in her hands. The leather was warm, like it was responding to her touch, and the symbol on the last page seemed to pulse faintly when she stared at it too long.

Luna, her grey tabby cat, jumped onto the desk, curling up beside her and purring contentedly. Ellie absentmindedly ran a finger through Luna's soft fur as she stared at the notebook. Her mind raced with possibilities. What was this thing? What was it for? Why had her grandmother kept it hidden?

Without thinking, she grabbed her pencil and began to sketch, letting her hand move instinctively across the page. Her eyes followed the lines she drew, each stroke feeling more deliberate, more sure of itself than usual. The drawing was of Luna, her cat's fur so meticulously captured that the drawing almost seemed to breathe with life.

Ellie paused for a moment, surprised by how effortlessly the drawing had come to life. The shading, the tiny details— everything had flowed from her pencil in a way it never had before. It was like the notebook was guiding her hand, filling her mind with ideas before she even had a chance to process them.

She flipped the page, the edges of her pencil scratching against the next clean sheet. This time, she didn't even hesitate. She began drawing again, but this time, the image wasn't of Luna. It was something bigger. Something strange. A vast forest, with towering trees and wild animals lurking in the shadows. It was wild and untamed, unlike anything she had ever seen before. Ellie felt a strange pull to it, as though she was standing in the middle of the forest herself. She could almost smell the earthy scent of the trees, feel the crisp air against her skin.

But then, something odd happened. As she finished the sketch, the lines on the paper began to shimmer, glowing faintly in the dim light. Ellie's breath caught in her throat. She stared at the drawing, unsure if she was imagining things. Suddenly, the air in the room grew thick. Ellie's heart raced as she watched in awe—and a little fear—as the scene she had drawn began to shift and change. The trees in the drawing seemed to stretch and twist, and the ground beneath them seemed to ripple like a living thing. A low growl echoed from the page, and Ellie jumped back in shock.

Luna hissed and arched her back, her fur standing on end as she leapt off the desk in alarm. Ellie's heart was pounding in her chest as she stared at the page, which now seemed to glow with an otherworldly energy. A dark shape began to emerge from the trees in the drawing, moving with unnatural speed.

The creature—some sort of shadowy beast—snarled, its glowing eyes locked onto Ellie. She gasped, her hand trembling as she reached for the notebook. But before she could even think to close it, the beast surged forward, leaping out of the drawing and into the air.

Ellie's scream caught in her throat as she leapt backward, nearly knocking over her lamp. The creature hovered in the air before her, its form shifting and changing, as if made of smoke and shadow. It let out another growl, this time louder, more threatening, and Ellie stumbled back in terror.

"Ellie, what's going on?" Daniel's voice cracked from the doorway, his footsteps hurried.

Ellie couldn't answer. She was too stunned to speak, her eyes fixed on the creature before her.

The beast let out a final roar and then, as quickly as it had appeared, it vanished back into the notebook. The glowing faded, and the room fell silent once again.

Ellie's pulse thudded in her ears as she stood frozen. The notebook lay there, ordinary once more. Luna cautiously approached and rubbed against her leg, purring softly as though nothing unusual had happened. But Ellie knew better. She wasn't imagining what had just occurred.

She had drawn something to life. Something dangerous.

"What is this thing?" she whispered, her fingers trembling as she reached for the notebook. She didn't know the answer yet.

The next day, Ellie could hardly focus on anything else. She went through the motions of helping Daniel pack for the weekend trip, but her mind was still on the strange events of the night before. How could something like that happen? How could a drawing come to life?

By lunchtime, she found herself pacing back and forth in her room, Luna curled up on her bed, still as calm as ever. Ellie sat down at her desk, the notebook staring back at her like it was daring her to open it again.

"Okay," she muttered to herself, "Let's try this again."

She carefully flipped the notebook open to a new page, her pencil hovering above it. She couldn't shake the feeling that the notebook was more than just a tool for drawing. It was something... alive. Something that could change the world around her.

She glanced over at Luna, who was watching her intently, as if she knew something Ellie didn't. Ellie hesitated for a moment, then put the pencil to the page. She started drawing again.

The pencil felt heavier than usual in Ellie's hand as she began to sketch. Her mind was a whirlwind of confusion and fear, still grappling with what had happened the night before. But beneath all that, a strange curiosity simmered, urging her to try again.

The first time she had drawn, it had been an accident. The beast had come from nowhere, a figment of her imagination made real. But this time—this time, she felt as if she was in control. She could make it happen again. She could control the magic of the notebook.

She set her jaw, determined to experiment. She would start with something simple. Her first impulse was to sketch Luna, her cat, just to see if the magic would repeat itself. She began with a few quick strokes, capturing Luna's sleek fur and calm eyes.

But as she drew, Ellie's mood shifted. The uncertainty that had gripped her since the night before returned, and with it came a tinge of frustration. *What am I doing?* she thought. *How is this possible?*

The lines of her drawing began to feel stiff, her pencil dragging across the page with more force than intended. Ellie's brow furrowed, her frustration mounting as she struggled to capture Luna's likeness just right.

As she pressed harder, the page beneath her pencil began to change colour. First, a soft shade of pale blue appeared in the areas where her hand touched the paper. Then, as her frustration deepened, the blue shifted into a swirling violet.

Ellie's heart skipped a beat. She pulled back for a moment,

staring at the page.

What...

The violet deepened, becoming darker, almost as if the paper

was absorbing her emotions. The swirls of colour seemed to

pulse in time with her heartbeat, and Ellie felt a strange energy

fill the room. It was like the notebook itself was responding to

her mood.

Luna, perched on the edge of the desk, blinked slowly at the

drawing. The cat's ears flicked back as she hissed softly, her

tail flicking in agitation. Ellie glanced up in surprise. Luna's

behaviour mirrored her own frustration. It was as if the room

was suffused with tension.

Then, to Ellie's shock, the page rippled. It was like the colour

had become liquid, swirling into the shape of something that

wasn't there before. Her pencil had drawn the outlines of

Luna, but the page had turned it into something... more. The drawing began to shimmer and warp before her eyes, and suddenly, Luna was no longer just a drawing on paper. A version of Luna—wild-eyed, with glowing green pupils—stepped out from the page, her fur bristling with an eerie energy. The cat didn't look like her pet anymore. She was more... untamed, more otherworldly.

Ellie recoiled, her hand shaking, the pencil slipping from her grasp and falling to the floor. Luna on the desk let out a low growl, and Ellie instinctively backed away. The version of Luna that had emerged from the page stared at her with a mix of curiosity and menace, its fur crackling with a faint blue glow, a reflection of the colour now pulsing on the page.

The creature—no, the *drawing*—tilted its head, as though sizing Ellie up. Then, with a flick of its tail, it disappeared back into the page, as quickly as it had come.

Ellie's breath came in sharp gasps as she stared at the now calm page. The swirling colours had receded, leaving the paper pristine once again. The faint glow remained, though, lingering in the air like a faint mist. She reached for the page with trembling fingers, almost afraid to touch it.

Luna, the real Luna, hopped off the desk and padded over to Ellie, rubbing against her leg, purring softly. The tension in the room slowly began to dissipate, but Ellie couldn't shake the feeling that something had changed—something inside the notebook, inside her.

"Okay, I get it," she whispered to herself. "It's... it's my emotions. The notebook can sense them."

She leaned back in her chair, her heart still racing. Her mind was a whirl of thoughts, each one trying to make sense of what had just happened. *Could this be real? Could this notebook actually...* She glanced down at the paper again, then at the faint, swirling glow that still lingered in the air. *I need to show this to someone.*

But who would believe her? She couldn't even fully comprehend what had just happened herself.

Ellie sighed and closed the notebook, careful to shut it gently, as though afraid it might explode with some new, unknown magic if she wasn't cautious. She leaned back in her chair and ran a hand through her hair, trying to calm the storm of emotions inside her. Her thoughts turned to her friends—Zara, Max, Theo, and Jake. Would they even believe her? They'd always thought she was a little too imaginative, a little too quiet. But this wasn't imagination. This was real.

Luna, sensing Ellie's turmoil, jumped onto her lap and curled up in a soft ball, her purring vibrating through Ellie's legs. It was a small comfort, but one that made Ellie smile despite herself.

The notebook was powerful, and it had a mind of its own. But what had it meant when it responded to her frustration? Was it going to respond to every emotion she felt from now on? What if it made something worse next time?

The weight of the notebook in her hands felt heavier now.
More dangerous. But in that weight, Ellie also felt something
else: possibility.

That afternoon, Ellie didn't touch the notebook again. Instead,
she let herself sink into her sketchbook—the one she'd found
in the loft weeks ago and forgotten about. She drew for hours,
her pencil gliding across the page, capturing everything from
the sun-dappled trees outside her window to the tiny, intricate
patterns in Luna's fur. She felt the familiar calmness of her
art, the way it allowed her to process everything swirling
inside her.

But when she looked up at the clock, she realised it was
getting late. The house was quiet now, with Daniel off running
errands for their mom. Ellie was alone with her thoughts, and
the strange events of the morning were never far from her
mind.

She glanced toward the notebook. Would it respond to her peaceful mood? Or was it always going to be tied to her emotions in unpredictable ways?

With a deep breath, Ellie opened the notebook again, determined to find out.

This time, the pages stayed blank. But as Ellie sketched lightly, the colours on the paper remained calm—no swirling purples, no fiery reds. Just a soft, gentle green that spread across the page as she drew. The colour seemed to soak into the paper like a quiet, calming breeze.

Her hand stilled as she realised that the notebook wasn't just reflecting her emotions—it was mirroring them. The more at peace she felt, the softer the magic became. And in that softness, Ellie understood something else: the notebook wasn't just a tool. It was a mirror.

And she wasn't sure if that was a good thing.

Chapter 2 – a Meeting of minds

The sunlight filtered softly through the curtains as Ellie sat at her desk, absently tracing the rim of her mug with her fingers. Her thoughts kept spiralling back to the notebook, its eerie power lingering in her mind like an unsolved mystery. The pages shifting with her emotions, the strange creatures and visions that emerged when her mood shifted... it was all too much for her to process alone.

Her eyes flicked to the clock. The others would be arriving soon—Zara, Max, Theo, and Jake. They'd all agreed to meet up for a late afternoon hangout at her place, but Ellie had a feeling today would be different. She wasn't just meeting them for a casual chat. No, this was something more urgent. She had to tell them about the notebook. But how? How could she explain what was happening without sounding completely insane?

Her hand hovered over the notebook, still resting on her desk. The leather cover looked so innocent, so calm. But she knew better now. She had felt its magic, its pulse beneath her fingers. She wasn't sure how to control it, or even if she *should*, but she had to know more. And the only way she could figure it out was by involving them.

As if on cue, a knock echoed at the door, followed by the voices of her friends. "Ellie, we're here!" Zara called out.

Ellie stood up, smoothing her shirt nervously as she made her way to the door. She swung it open, smiling at the group of teenagers who piled into the living room, each one with their unique flair.

Zara gave Ellie a knowing look. She had always been the type to analyse everything, and Ellie could tell her friend was already picking up on the tension in the air. Max followed her in, adjusting his glasses and looking slightly anxious, as usual. He was always the realist, the one who would ask the hard questions. Theo sauntered in behind them, arms crossed, the sceptical look on his face already in place. And Jake—well, Jake was as unpredictable as ever, grinning like he'd just won a prize he hadn't been expecting.

"Alright, what's going on, Ellie?" Zara asked, eyes narrowing slightly. "You sounded... strange on the phone."

Ellie swallowed, her stomach twisting. She wasn't sure how to begin. But she couldn't keep this to herself anymore. She had to tell them. They were her closest friends. She trusted them.

"Okay, um..." Ellie began, her voice shaking slightly as she sat down on the couch. Luna, her grey tabby, jumped into her lap, sensing Ellie's anxiety. "I... I found something in the loft a few days ago."

The group gathered around her, curious but wary.

Ellie hesitated, but then, remembering how she had felt the notebook's magic, she knew she couldn't hold back. "I found this old notebook, and... I think it has some kind of magic in it."

Zara raised an eyebrow, the scepticism evident in her eyes. "Magic? Seriously? Ellie, are you okay? You sound like you're in one of those books you always read."

"I know it sounds crazy," Ellie said quickly, cutting her off. "But I swear, it's real. The pages... they change. They respond to my emotions."

"Wait, what?" Max blinked, adjusting his glasses, his voice barely above a whisper. "How does that even work?"

Ellie took a deep breath. "I drew something in it. Just a picture of Luna, at first, but when I got frustrated, the page turned this weird colour. And then... the picture, the drawing, came to life."

The room fell silent. The others exchanged glances, unsure of what to make of it.

"Are you serious right now?" Theo's voice was low, his tone more disbelieving than before. "You're saying your drawing... *came to life*? Like some kind of... magic portal or something?"

Ellie nodded, her fingers clutching the notebook on her lap.

"Yeah. I know how it sounds, but it really happened. I don't know how or why, but I think the notebook has something to do with my emotions. When I get frustrated or upset, the page changes colour. And whatever I draw seems to... react to it. I'm not sure what the rules are, but I need help figuring it out."

Jake, who had been leaning back casually in his chair, suddenly sat up with a mischievous grin plastered on his face. "Wait, hold up. So, let me get this straight," he began, his voice full of mock seriousness. "You're telling me that *this* book can make stuff come to life if you draw it, like a magic sketchbook? And if you're frustrated, your drawings turn into, what, monsters?"

Ellie nodded, her expression tense but also a little amused by Jake's dramatic flair. "Pretty much."

Jake threw his hands up in the air, feigning shock. "This is the best thing I've heard all week! I mean, who needs a boring old TV when you can literally *draw* your own action-packed adventures?" He paused for a beat, looking around at the group. "Think about it. We could get a pet dragon. Or a pet ninja. Maybe even a pet superhero. This is my dream come true."

Zara rolled her eyes, her tone sharp. "Jake, not everything needs to be a joke. This is serious. Ellie could've unleashed something dangerous with that notebook."

Jake just grinned, unphased. "Oh, come on, Zara. You can't tell me you're not curious about what kind of trouble we could get into with this thing. I mean, who's *really* going to say no to a dragon?"

Max adjusted his glasses, still looking a bit uneasy. "We're not here to have fun with this, Jake. We're talking about something that could go horribly wrong. What if it gets out of control?"

"I get it, Max," Ellie said, holding up her hands. "I'm not saying we should go crazy with it. I just need to understand what's happening first. And I don't want to do it alone."

47

Theo, who had been quietly observing, spoke up, his voice cold but thoughtful. "So, the notebook responds to your emotions... but what happens if it's not just you using it? What if someone else draws in it? Do we risk it doing something *worse*?"

Ellie bit her lip. "That's what I'm scared of. I don't know what the limits are. Or if there even *are* any limits."

Jake suddenly leaned forward, looking much more serious than usual. "Okay, okay, I get it. No dragons or ninjas... for now." He flashed a mischievous grin, but his tone softened. "But seriously, I think we need to try it out. We need to understand it. You can't just keep it locked up, afraid to use it. Let's figure out what it can really do. Together."

Zara met Ellie's eyes, her expression still serious, but there was a flicker of understanding there. "Jake's right. If we're going to help you, we need to see it for ourselves. But we're doing it carefully. No 'pet dragons,' okay?"

"Deal," Jake said, hands raised in mock surrender.

Ellie felt a weight lift from her chest. For all their teasing and joking around, her friends were here for her. They were in this together, no matter how weird or dangerous it might get. With a deep breath, Ellie opened the notebook again. She glanced at Luna, who was watching the group curiously from her spot on Ellie's lap. "Alright," she said, feeling a mix of nerves and excitement. "Let's see what happens."

Chapter 3 – Notebook rules

The room was quiet, the only sounds being the occasional rustle of pages as Ellie flipped through the notebook. Her heart was pounding, anticipation and uncertainty swirling in her chest. The group sat around her, all eyes fixed on the open book in front of her. The magic was undeniable, and now it was time to figure out the rules.

"So," Jake said, breaking the silence. "What now? Do we just start drawing and see what happens?"

Ellie looked up from the notebook, her fingers still grazing the edges of the pages. "I don't think it's that simple," she said, her voice quieter than usual. "I think there's more to it. I've tried drawing in it a few times now, but I still don't understand why it changes colours, or what makes it do that."

Zara leaned forward, her arms crossed as she scrutinised the notebook. "You said it reacts to your emotions, right? Maybe there's a pattern to it. Maybe it's not random." Her voice was calm, analytical, but Ellie could sense the undercurrent of curiosity in her tone.

Max adjusted his glasses, looking anxious. "What if it's not just emotions? What if there's something else in play here? Like… like a trigger or a specific action?"

Ellie nodded slowly. "I thought about that. But I'm not sure what it is. Sometimes the page turns colours when I get frustrated, sometimes when I'm happy… It's unpredictable."

Theo, who had been silent up until now, spoke up, his voice laced with doubt. "So, you're telling me that this notebook changes colour based on how you feel, and then things… come to life?" He shook his head. "Sounds like a recipe for disaster."

"I know," Ellie replied, a sigh escaping her lips. "That's why I need to figure out the rules. I don't want to make anything worse."

Jake, who had been fidgeting with his sleeves, grinned mischievously. "What's the worst that could happen? You

51

accidentally draw a dragon that burns your house down? I mean, that would be kind of cool."

"Jake," Zara said sharply, her voice firm. "This isn't a joke. If something goes wrong—"

"I know, I know," Jake said, raising his hands in mock surrender. "I'm just saying, it's a good thing we're all in this together, right?"

Ellie nodded, feeling a flicker of gratitude. She knew that despite Jake's jokes, he was right. They were in this together, and they would figure it out. But it wasn't going to be easy.

"Alright," she said, taking a deep breath. "Let's start by testing things out carefully. I don't want to risk drawing something that could go out of control. We'll try it slowly and see what happens."

Zara raised an eyebrow. "Slowly? You mean like... a sketch of a flower or something?"

Ellie smiled faintly. "Yeah. Something simple."

Theo leaned back in his chair, crossing his arms again. "And how exactly do you plan on triggering the notebook? Do you just sit there and wait until you're in the right mood?"

Ellie thought for a moment. "I don't think I have to wait. When I was drawing Luna the other day, I was just... I don't know... focused. And I didn't even notice when the page started changing. It was like it was reacting to my thoughts or energy, not just my emotions."

Max leaned in, his expression serious. "So, you think the notebook is, like, attuned to your mental state, not just your feelings?"

"I think so," Ellie said, feeling more confident as she spoke. "It's not just about being happy or sad. It's about... what's going on inside me at that moment."

Zara nodded thoughtfully. "Okay. So, we'll need to observe the notebook carefully and see if there's a pattern. If we're going to test this, we need to be methodical."

Ellie took the notebook and turned to a blank page. She

hesitated for a moment, feeling the weight of her decision.

This wasn't just some ordinary sketchbook. It had a life of its

own, and she wasn't sure what the consequences of using it

carelessly would be.

"Alright," she said, taking a deep breath. "Let's see what

happens."

She picked up a pen and started to sketch a simple outline of

a tree. It was nothing special—just a rough drawing of a tree

with a few branches. As she drew, she tried to focus her mind,

clearing away all other thoughts and letting herself be

absorbed in the process.

The others watched in silence, their eyes fixed on her as she

worked. Ellie's hand moved across the page with ease, the

lines flowing smoothly. But as she finished the outline of the

tree, she noticed something strange. The edges of the page

had begun to change colour—faint streaks of green were

appearing along the edges.

She froze, staring at the page. The green deepened, swirling in intricate patterns, and Ellie's heart raced. She hadn't been expecting this. The tree she'd drawn seemed to be reacting to something—something beyond her control.

"What's happening?" Max whispered, his voice trembling slightly. "Is it... is it supposed to do that?"

Ellie didn't answer immediately. She was too focused on the notebook, watching as the green spread across the page, then deepened into a vibrant emerald hue. The branches of the tree began to shift, almost as if they were stretching, reaching for the edges of the paper.

The room was still, everyone waiting for something to happen. Ellie's pulse quickened, unsure whether to be excited or terrified.

Then, with a soft rustling sound, the tree in the notebook seemed to *breathe*. The branches flexed, the leaves rustling as if a breeze had passed through them. The notebook hummed gently, a low, soothing vibration that seemed to fill the room.

"It's... alive," Theo muttered, his eyes wide.

Ellie couldn't speak. Her mind was racing, trying to process what she was seeing. The tree had come to life, but it wasn't a wild, dangerous thing. It was... calm. Peaceful, even.

"What do we do now?" Zara asked, her voice barely above a whisper.

Ellie slowly reached out and touched the page, her fingers brushing the tree's branches. They felt soft and delicate, but with a strange energy pulsing through them. The moment her fingers made contact, the tree seemed to respond, the leaves shifting as if they recognised her touch.

"I... I think it's okay," Ellie said, her voice soft. "It's not hurting anything."

Jake, who had been watching with a mixture of disbelief and excitement, leaned forward. "Okay, now this is officially the coolest thing ever. Can I try? What if I draw something even bigger, like a dragon or—"

"Jake!" Zara snapped, glaring at him. "We're not going to just experiment with it like that. We need to be careful."

Ellie nodded, still absorbed in the sight of the tree. "Zara's right. We need to figure out what makes it react this way before we try anything else. This could be dangerous if we don't understand it."

Max adjusted his glasses. "So, we've learned one thing: the notebook is sensitive to your mental focus, not just your emotions. But it seems like there's more to it. We need to figure out the *rules* before we get too carried away."

"Yeah," Jake said, sitting back with a grin. "Definitely no pet dragons. Not yet anyway."

Ellie closed the notebook slowly, the tree fading back into the pages. She took a deep breath, feeling a mix of awe and apprehension. They had just scratched the surface. But there were rules to be discovered—and she was determined to figure them out.

"Let's keep testing it," she said, her voice steady now. "But no rushing. We'll take it one step at a time."

The room was quiet again, the group still absorbed in the aftermaths of the tree's magical awakening. Ellie couldn't shake the feeling that there was more to the notebook—something deeper, something darker—that she hadn't discovered yet. The tree had been beautiful, calming even, but she knew it wasn't the only power it held. She had felt it in the way the notebook pulsed under her fingers, as if there were untold possibilities waiting to unfold.

The others had fallen into a hush, still processing the strange event. Jake was the first to speak.

"So, what now?" he asked, his voice light-hearted but carrying an undercurrent of excitement. "Do we just keep playing with the magic, or what?"

Ellie closed the notebook slowly, her fingers lingering on the edge of the cover. "I don't know. But we need to be careful. That tree was harmless... but we can't be sure the notebook won't do something more dangerous."

Zara nodded, her gaze thoughtful. "I agree. We don't fully understand how this thing works, so we should approach it with caution. But we're not going to figure it out by sitting here doing nothing."

Max shifted uncomfortably in his chair. "Yeah, but what if the magic is... unpredictable? What if it's not just about drawing things? What if writing in it changes the outcome?"

Ellie raised an eyebrow, intrigued by the suggestion. "What do you mean?"

Max hesitated, adjusting his glasses nervously. "I don't know... like, maybe the notebook reacts to words, too? Not just pictures. If you wrote something in it—like a wish—what would happen?"

The words sent a chill down Ellie's spine. She wasn't sure she was ready to test something like that. Wishes… they sounded so simple, but she had a feeling they weren't. There had to be a catch.

"You think that if we wrote 'I wish' in it, it would come true?" Zara asked, her voice sceptical but tinged with curiosity.

Max shrugged, looking more nervous by the second. "I mean, what if it does? This thing is full of strange magic. It could be possible."

Theo spoke up from across the room, his voice quieter than usual. "I wouldn't mess with that. Wishing for something sounds like the kind of thing that always comes with a cost."

Ellie stared at the notebook, her mind racing. She'd always been careful with her wishes. Her mom used to tell her that wishes were tricky things—they had a way of coming true when you least expected them, but never exactly how you imagined. But this was different. This wasn't some childhood superstition. This was really magic. And the more she thought

60

about it, the more she realised that whatever it was, it couldn't be as simple as writing down a wish.

"I think we should try it," Jake said suddenly, his voice playful.

"I mean, what's the worst that could happen?"

Zara shot him a look. "Don't be reckless."

Jake just grinned. "No, seriously. We all want something, right? Why not test it out and see what happens?"

Max shook his head, his voice growing more anxious. "But what if there's a *bad* side to it? Like, what if—"

Before Max could finish his sentence, Jake grabbed a pen, flipped open the notebook, and wrote on a blank page with dramatic flair. Ellie's eyes widened as she saw the words: *I wish to be the happiest person alive.*

The air in the room seemed to grow thicker as everyone leaned in, watching Jake's words take shape on the page. Ellie felt a strange tension coil in her chest as the notebook vibrated lightly under Jake's hand. She had been afraid of this, of someone tempting fate with a simple wish.

"What did you do?" Ellie asked, her voice tight with worry.

Jake laughed, clearly unfazed. "Relax. I'm just testing it out."

As if on cue, the words on the page began to glow, the ink shimmering with a faint golden light. The light grew brighter and brighter, enveloping the page. Then, in a flash, it was gone.

Jake blinked, his grin widening. "Whoa. That was—"

But before he could finish his sentence, his expression shifted. A strange feeling seemed to fill the room, a sudden rush of warmth flooding over him. His eyes sparkled, his lips curved into an even wider smile. He practically radiated happiness, as though he had just won a lottery he hadn't even entered.

"I feel... amazing," Jake said, his voice bubbling with excitement. "This is incredible! I've never felt this good in my life!"

The others exchanged confused looks, but no one had time to ask what was happening before Ellie suddenly felt something shift inside her. A heavy, sinking sensation washed over her. Her stomach churned, and her mind clouded with an overwhelming wave of sadness, as if the world had suddenly lost all its colour.

She looked at the others, her heart racing. "What's going on?" she whispered, barely able to keep her voice steady.

Max, who had been quiet until now, suddenly gasped. His face had gone pale, and his hands were shaking as he sat frozen in his seat.

"It's happening to *me*, too," he said, his voice barely audible. "I... I feel so... so empty. Like there's nothing left inside me."

Ellie's eyes widened in horror. She could feel the weight of the sadness creeping into her chest, tightening her throat, and making it hard to breathe. But it wasn't just her. It was Max, too. Something was wrong. The magic hadn't just affected Jake—it had shifted the balance, creating an opposite reaction in someone else.

Jake, still basking in his happiness, didn't seem to notice the change. He stood up, a wild grin on his face. "This is it, guys. This is the best thing ever!"

But Ellie could barely focus on him. She could feel the emotional toll hitting Max even harder. His face was pale, his eyes dull, as if the joy that had radiated from him just moments ago had been drained away.

"I don't feel... right," Max said, his voice trembling. "Ellie, what happened? Why do I feel so—"

Before he could finish, a cold shiver ran down Ellie's spine. The room seemed to shift again, and she realised with a sinking feeling that what had just happened wasn't a coincidence.

Jake's wish had come true—he was on top of the world, filled with a happiness that seemed to have no end. But someone else had to pay the price. Max, who had been sitting closest to him, had been the one to feel the weight of the magic's consequence. His happiness had been siphoned away, replaced by a deep, soul-crushing sadness that felt like it was never going to end.

Ellie felt a wave of guilt rush over her. She hadn't been the one to make the wish, but she felt responsible for what was happening. There was no way Jake could know the consequences of his actions.

"You…" Ellie started, her voice shaking. "You must take it back. You must wish it away."

Jake stopped mid-step, his grin faltering as he looked at Ellie, his eyes finally flicking to Max. "Wait, what happened to him?" He turned back to the notebook, but Ellie stopped him before he could write again.

"No," she said firmly. "We can't just keep using it like this. The magic isn't something you can control. There's always a cost. We need to find a way to reverse it."

Zara, who had been quiet until now, stood up. "This is what happens when you mess with things you don't understand," she said, her tone sharp. "If we can't undo what's been done, but we need to figure out how to balance it. We can't let this get out of control."

Ellie closed her eyes, feeling the weight of the situation settle in. The notebook wasn't just a tool for creating or drawing—it had the power to grant wishes. But as they had learned the hard way, every wish came with a price. And they would have to be incredibly careful, or the consequences could be far worse than they could ever imagine.

The room buzzed with tension. Max sat slumped in his chair, his head in his hands, while Jake paced nervously, the joy in his expression slowly giving way to guilt. Ellie, Zara, and Theo exchanged uneasy glances, the weight of the situation settling over them like a storm cloud.

"Okay," Zara began, breaking the silence, "we need to figure out how to reverse this. Max can't stay like this—it's not fair."

Jake stopped pacing, rubbing the back of his neck awkwardly. "I didn't know it would... you know, hurt anyone," he said, his voice uncharacteristically subdued. "I just thought it was a cool idea."

Ellie shot him a look that was equal parts frustration and pity. "Magic doesn't work like that. It's never just one thing. There's always a balance. If the notebook made you this happy, it had to take it from somewhere."

Theo, leaning against the wall with his arms crossed, spoke up. "So how do we fix it? Another wish? What if that makes things worse?"

"That's the problem," Zara said, her voice firm. "We don't know how this works yet. Making another wish without understanding the consequences could just mess things up more."

Ellie nodded, her mind racing. She glanced at the notebook, which now sat closed on the table. It looked so innocent, yet she knew it held a power far beyond their control. "Maybe we should start by writing in it again, but not a wish. Something to figure out the rules."

"Like what?" Jake asked, his brow furrowed.

Ellie thought for a moment. "We could try asking it something. Maybe it'll give us a clue."

Zara frowned. "That's risky. What if it twists the answer?"

Ellie hesitated but shook her head. "It's a chance we'll have to take. We can't leave Max like this."

Max lifted his head slowly, his voice hoarse. "I don't want you to risk it for me. What if it hurts someone else?"

"It won't," Ellie said firmly, though she wasn't entirely sure. "We'll be careful."

Ellie flipped open the notebook, her hand trembling slightly as she picked up a pen. The others crowded around her, their faces tense with anticipation. She turned to a blank page and, after a moment's hesitation, wrote:

How can we undo the wish?

The ink shimmered briefly, the letters seeming to sink into the page before vanishing entirely. For a few seconds, nothing happened. Then, slowly, new words began to appear in the same shimmering ink.

Every wish has its price. Balance must be restored.

"What does that even mean?" Jake asked, leaning over Ellie's shoulder to read the words.

"It means the magic doesn't work for free," Theo said, his voice heavy with scepticism. "If Jake got happiness, someone else had to lose it."

Zara's frown deepened. "So, if we want to fix this, we need to find a way to restore the balance."

"But how?" Ellie asked, her frustration mounting. "Do we just… write that we want to balance it out? Or is there something else we're supposed to do?"

Max let out a shuddering sigh. "What if… what if I'm supposed to give something up? To even things out?"

"No way," Ellie said firmly. "You didn't ask for this. Jake made the wish; it's not your fault."

Jake winced, the guilt on his face deepening. "I didn't mean to mess everything up. I'll fix it. I'll write something."

"Hold on," Zara said sharply, grabbing his arm before he could reach for the pen. "We can't rush this. If you write something without thinking it through, it could make things worse."

Jake pulled his arm back, looking frustrated. "So, what do we do? Sit here and hope it fixes itself?"

Ellie stared at the notebook, her mind racing. The words on the page echoed in her head: *Balance must be restored.* What did that mean? Could they force the magic to undo itself? Or was there something more they were missing?

"We need more information," Ellie said finally. "If the notebook responds to questions, maybe we can ask it how to restore balance without hurting anyone."

This time, Ellie wrote carefully, her hand steady despite the fear swirling inside her.

How can we restore balance without causing harm?

The notebook responded almost immediately, the ink shimmering and shifting as new words appeared.

To give, one must take. To take, one must give. The choice lies within.

Jake groaned, throwing his hands in the air. "What is this, some kind of riddle? Why can't it just tell us what to do?"

"Because magic doesn't work like that," Zara said, her voice sharp. "It's not going to hand us an easy answer."

Theo leaned closer to the notebook, his expression unreadable. "It's telling us we need to make a choice. Whatever we do to fix this, it's going to cost something."

Ellie swallowed hard, her mind spinning. The notebook wasn't going to give them a simple solution. Whatever balance they restored, it would require a sacrifice. But what could they give up that wouldn't hurt someone else?

"Maybe we can share the burden," Ellie said quietly. "If we all contribute something—time, energy, emotions—it might be enough to fix it without hurting anyone too badly."

71

Zara nodded slowly. "That could work. But we need to be sure before we try."

Jake stepped forward, determination in his eyes. "I made the wish. I'll take the hit. Whatever it takes to fix this, I'll do it."

"No," Ellie said, her voice firm. "We're in this together. We'll figure it out, but we'll do it as a team."

The group spent hours discussing possibilities, testing small experiments with the notebook to understand its magic. As they worked, Ellie couldn't shake the feeling that the notebook wasn't just a tool—it was testing them, forcing them to confront their own strengths and weaknesses.

By the time they reached a decision, the room was filled with an unspoken bond of trust. They had learned one thing for certain: the notebook's magic was powerful, but it was also dangerous. And if they were going to continue using it, they would need to understand its rules—and its consequences— far better than they did now.

Their plan was simple but risky: they would write one final message, asking to share the burden of restoring balance among all five of them. It wasn't a perfect solution, but it was their best chance at fixing the damage without causing more harm.

As Ellie pressed the pen to the page, she felt a strange sense of calm wash over her. The notebook's power was frightening, but it had also brought them together. And as she wrote the final words, she knew they were ready to face whatever came next—together.

Ellie's hand trembled as she finished writing the sentence in the notebook. Her words shimmered on the page, faint and glowing like the last light of a fading sunset:

Let the burden of balance be shared equally among the five of us.

The ink sank into the paper, disappearing as the notebook began to vibrate faintly. Everyone stepped back instinctively, the air around them suddenly feeling heavier. A faint, golden glow emanated from the notebook, growing brighter until the room seemed bathed in warm light.

"What's happening?" Jake asked, his voice tinged with both awe and fear.

"I don't know," Ellie replied, shielding her eyes from the glow. "Just stay calm. It's working—at least, I think it is."

The light grew brighter, pulsing in waves that seemed to resonate deep within each of them. Then, as suddenly as it had started, the glow faded, leaving the room eerily quiet. The group exchanged uneasy glances.

"Did it work?" Zara asked, her voice steady but cautious.

Jake opened his mouth to reply, but before he could speak, an overwhelming wave of emotion surged through the room. Ellie gasped, clutching her chest as a strange mix of happiness and sadness flooded her senses. She felt euphoric for a moment, then deeply melancholic, as though every high and low she'd ever experienced was hitting her all at once.

The others seemed to be feeling it, too. Jake clutched the edge of the table, his usual bravado replaced with wide-eyed confusion. Zara stumbled back, pressing a hand to her forehead. Theo leaned heavily against the wall, his usual stoic expression replaced with one of vulnerability. Max, who had been slumped in despair earlier, sat up straighter, his eyes bright with a tentative hope.

"I feel... everything," Ellie whispered, tears streaming down her face. "It's like... like the emotions are balancing themselves out."

Jake let out a shaky laugh, though it was tinged with unease. "Yeah, no kidding. This is... intense."

Zara straightened, her breathing steadying as she tried to make sense of what was happening. "It's like the happiness Jake wished for is being spread out across all of us. But so is the sadness. It's evening out."

As the intensity of the emotions began to fade, Ellie felt something else—a strange, subtle connection to the others. It was as though the notebook's magic had created a bond between them, something deeper than mere friendship. She could sense their emotions in a way she never had before, as if their hearts were beating in unison.

"Does anyone else... feel that?" Max asked hesitantly.

"Yeah," Theo muttered, looking down at his hands. "It's like I can feel what you're feeling. All of you."

Jake nodded, his usual grin replaced with a more subdued expression. "It's weird, but... kind of cool? Like, we're all linked now."

Ellie's mind raced as she tried to process the implications. The notebook's magic had restored balance, but it had done so by tying their emotions together. Whatever one of them felt, the others would feel, too—at least to some degree.

"This might actually be a good thing," Zara said, her tone thoughtful. "If we're connected like this, it could help us work together. We'll know when one of us is struggling, and we can support each other."

"But what if it becomes too much?" Max asked, his voice tinged with worry. "What if one of us feels something strong? Will it overwhelm the rest of us?"

Ellie glanced at the notebook, still lying innocently on the table. "I don't think the magic works that way," she said. "It seems to balance things out. If one of us feels something extreme, the others might share the weight so it's not as overwhelming."

To test the theory, Jake suggested an experiment. "Okay, let's see how this works," he said, his tone lighter now. "Everyone think of something happy—like, really happy. Let's see if it spreads."

Ellie closed her eyes, focusing on a memory of Luna, her grey tabby, curling up in her lap on a rainy afternoon. The warmth of the memory filled her chest, and she felt a faint ripple of happiness radiate outward.

The others must have felt it, too, because Jake suddenly grinned. "Hey, that's nice. Who's got the cat memory? That's good stuff."

Ellie opened her eyes, smiling despite herself. "That was me."

Zara nodded, her own smile small but genuine. "It's subtle, but I can feel it. Like a little boost of happiness."

Theo, ever the sceptic, crossed his arms. "Okay, but what about the bad stuff? What happens if someone's upset?"

The mood in the room shifted immediately. Ellie could sense Theo's unease, the flicker of doubt and discomfort he was trying to hide. The connection amplified it, spreading a faint tension among the group.

"Okay, okay, stop thinking bad thoughts!" Jake said quickly, waving his hands as if to dispel the mood. "We get it—it works both ways."

As the group settled down, the reality of their new connection began to sink in. The notebook's magic had solved the immediate problem, but it had also created a new challenge. They were bound together now, their emotions intertwined in ways that would require patience, understanding, and trust.

"It's not just about us anymore," Ellie said softly. "Whatever we feel, it affects everyone else. We must be careful."

Zara nodded, her expression serious. "This is a responsibility. We need to think about how we use this connection—and how we use the notebook. If we're not careful, we could hurt each other without meaning to."

Jake, ever the joker, gave a lopsided grin. "Well, at least we've got a built-in mood detector now. No more hiding how we feel, right?"

Despite the weight of the situation, Ellie found herself smiling. Jake's humour was a small but welcome relief, a reminder that they could face whatever came next together.

As they sat together, the notebook glowing faintly on the table between them, Ellie couldn't shake the feeling that this was only the beginning. The notebook's magic was powerful, unpredictable, and dangerous.

The days that followed were eerily quiet. After their intense experience with the notebook, the group had collectively decided to put it aside, at least for a while. They needed space—to process, to reflect, and maybe even to feel normal again.

Ellie tucked the notebook away in a drawer in her desk, sliding it under her sketchpad and a small stack of unfinished drawings. Out of sight, out of mind—or so she hoped.

For the first time in weeks, life began to feel ordinary again. The shared emotional connection that had tied them together so strongly after their last experiment had started to fade. It wasn't gone entirely—Ellie could still sense faint echoes of the others' emotions now and then—but the intensity had diminished to something manageable, almost imperceptible.

Ellie sat cross-legged on her bedroom floor, Luna purring softly in her lap. She ran her fingers through the cat's grey fur, her thoughts drifting back to the notebook. Despite everything that had happened, a small part of her missed the connection they'd shared. It had been overwhelming, yes, but it had also made her feel closer to the others than ever before.

She glanced at her sketchpad, flipping it open to a half-finished drawing of the notebook. She picked up her pencil, shading the edges and adding a faint glow around it, as though it radiated an otherworldly energy. "I wonder if we'll ever really understand you," she whispered.

Zara threw herself into her usual routines—school, soccer practice, tutoring sessions—anything to keep her mind occupied. She told herself she wasn't avoiding the notebook; she was just being practical.

But in the quiet moments, when she was alone in her room or walking home from practice, her thoughts inevitably returned to it. The experience had shaken her more than she cared to admit. She prided herself on being logical and level-headed, but the notebook's magic had defied all reason.

Every wish has its price. The words echoed in her mind like a warning. She couldn't shake the feeling that they were only beginning to scratch the surface of what the notebook was capable of—and that its magic was far more dangerous than they realised.

Jake, on the other hand, tried his best to pretend the notebook didn't exist. He focused on cracking jokes, hanging out with friends, and avoiding anything remotely serious. But late at night, when he was lying in bed staring at the ceiling, the guilt crept back in.

His wish had hurt Max, and even though they'd fixed it, he couldn't help but wonder what might have happened if the group hadn't stepped in.

"I'm not going to mess it up again," he muttered to himself, as if saying it out loud would make it true.

Still, a tiny part of him couldn't help but be tempted. The notebook was powerful, and he couldn't shake the thought of what else it might be able to do.

Max was relieved that things had returned to normal—or as normal as they could be after everything that had happened. The crushing despair he'd felt after Jake's wish had faded, leaving him feeling like himself again.

But the experience had left a mark. He found himself second-guessing everything, wondering what invisible forces might be at play behind even the smallest decisions. The notebook had shown him how fragile happiness could be—and how easily it could be taken away.

Still, he was grateful for the group.

Theo spent most of his time alone, as usual. He didn't like to dwell on the past, but the notebook lingered in the back of his mind like an itch he couldn't scratch.

He hated the way it had made him feel—vulnerable, exposed. The connection they'd shared had been both a blessing and a curse, forcing him to confront emotions he'd rather keep buried.

But despite his reservations, Theo couldn't deny that the notebook fascinated him. He'd always been drawn to mysteries, and the notebook was the biggest mystery of all.

As the days turned into weeks, the group's shared emotional connection continued to fade, until it was little more than a faint whisper in the background of their minds. Life returned to its usual rhythms, and the notebook remained untouched.

But each of them knew, deep down, that this was only a temporary reprieve. The notebook wasn't done with them—not by a long shot.

Chapter 4 – Pet whispers

Ellie woke to the gentle vibrations of Luna purring on her chest, the grey tabby nestled against her as though seeking refuge from a distant storm. The early morning light streamed through her curtains, painting golden streaks across her room. Stretching, Ellie scratched behind Luna's ears, earning a pleased chirrup in response.

"Morning, Luna," Ellie murmured, rubbing the sleep from her eyes. "Did you sleep well?"

The cat blinked at her, slow and deliberate, as if to say, *better than you, apparently.*

Ellie smiled and swung her legs over the side of the bed. She had just begun to tie her hair back when something odd caught her attention. Luna was staring at her—not in the usual way cats do, but with an intensity that felt almost... purposeful.

"Something on your mind?" Ellie asked with a chuckle, expecting no response.

To her utter astonishment, a faint, whispery voice brushed against her thoughts.

"You shouldn't have trusted the notebook."

Ellie froze, her hands hovering mid-air. "What?" she whispered aloud, her heart pounding in her chest. She looked down at Luna, who gazed back at her with calm, unblinking eyes.

The voice came again, faint but unmistakable.

"The balance isn't perfect. There's always a cost."

Ellie's pulse quickened as she tried to make sense of what she was hearing. "Luna... are you... talking?"

The cat stretched lazily, as if unimpressed by her human's astonishment. The voice echoed once more, softer this time.

"Not exactly. You're hearing what I want you to know."

Ellie stumbled back onto her bed, clutching the blankets as though they might ground her. She had always known the notebook's magic was strange and unpredictable, but this was something else entirely. Could it have awakened a connection between her and Luna?

She didn't have time to dwell on it, because Luna padded closer, brushing her head against Ellie's arm.

"It's not just me," the voice continued. "The others... their pets are starting to sense it, too."

"The others?" Ellie whispered.

Luna blinked slowly, her gaze steady. "The ones you share the bond with. Pay attention. We've always been watching."

Across town, Max was sitting in his backyard with Baxter, his cheerful golden retriever, who was bounding around with his favourite tennis ball. Despite the clear blue sky and the pleasant warmth of the day, Max felt uneasy.

"Baxter," he said, tossing the ball absentmindedly, "you ever feel like something's... off?"

Baxter trotted back, tail wagging, and dropped the ball at Max's feet. For a moment, Max swore he heard a faint chuckle—light-hearted and playful, just like his dog.

"You're overthinking, as usual," a warm voice seemed to say.

Max froze, his eyes darting to Baxter, who was now lying on the grass, panting happily.

"Did you just...?" Max started, then shook his head. "No way. I'm losing it."

But as Baxter wagged his tail, Max felt a strange sense of reassurance, as though the dog was telling him, *You're not alone.*

Zara had just finished soccer practice and was walking home with Trixie, her sleek black cat, who often followed her on short walks. The notebook was the last thing she wanted to think about, but her mind kept circling back to it.

As they neared her house, Trixie darted ahead, leaping onto a nearby railing and staring intently at Zara.

"What's up, Trix?" Zara asked, unlocking the door.

"Don't ignore it," a voice whispered, low and steady.

Zara froze mid-step, her eyes narrowing at the cat. "What did you just say?"

Trixie tilted her head, her green eyes glinting.

The voice came again, softer this time. "You'll need to face it sooner or later."

Zara shook her head, pushing the door open. "Great. Now I'm imagining things."

But deep down, she couldn't shake the feeling that Trixie knew something she didn't.

Jake was sprawled on the couch, tossing popcorn into the air and catching it in his mouth. Milo, his mischievous ferret, scurried across the coffee table, sniffing at the bowl.

"Don't even think about it," Jake said, pointing at Milo with mock seriousness.

The ferret paused, looking up at him with wide, curious eyes.

Then Jake heard it—a soft, cheeky whisper.

"You're no fun."

Jake nearly choked on his popcorn. "Whoa, hold on. Did you just...?"

Milo chittered, darting around the table as if laughing at Jake's reaction.

Jake shook his head, grinning despite himself. "Okay, this is either the notebook's doing, or I've officially lost my mind."

Theo sat alone in his room, scribbling notes in the margins of a book while Shadow, his sleek greyhound, lay curled up on the rug. The quiet was comforting, a welcome break from the chaos of the past few weeks.

But then Shadow lifted her head, her ears twitching. She stared at Theo with an intensity that made him pause.

"What is it, girl?" he asked, lowering his pen.

The answer came not in barks or whines, but in a low, thoughtful whisper. *"You're not as alone as you think."*

Theo stiffened, his eyes narrowing at the dog. "Did you just... talk to me?"

Shadow's tail thumped once against the rug. Theo leaned back in his chair, his mind racing.

It didn't take long for the group to realise that something strange was happening. One by one, they reached out to each other, sharing their experiences with their pets.

"Okay, so it's not just me," Ellie said during their next meeting, Luna perched calmly on her lap.

"Nope," Jake replied, Milo peeking out of his hoodie pocket. "Either we've all gone crazy, or the notebook's magic has rubbed off on our pets."

"It makes sense, in a weird way," Zara said, stroking Trixie, who purred contentedly in her arms. "The notebook tied us together, so maybe it's extending to the ones closest to us."

Theo crossed his arms, glancing down at Shadow, who sat at his feet. "If this is permanent, we're going to have to figure out how to deal with it."

Max nodded, scratching Baxter behind the ears. "And what it means. This can't be a coincidence."

Ellie looked around at the group, her heart swelling with a strange mix of apprehension and hope. The notebook's magic was unpredictable, but maybe, just maybe, their pets were the key to understanding it.

Chapter 5 – The decision

The group gathered in Zara's basement, the usual meeting spot for serious discussions. The space was dimly lit, the only source of light a warm desk lamp in the corner, which cast long shadows on the walls. The notebook sat in the centre of the low coffee table, its cover unassuming yet charged with an invisible weight.

No one wanted to be the first to speak.

Ellie broke the silence, her voice hesitant. "We can't keep ignoring it. The notebook's not going to go away on its own."

Jake leaned back in his chair, hands behind his head. "Well, destroying it would solve that problem, wouldn't it?" His tone was light, but his words hung heavily in the air.

Zara frowned, her arms crossed tightly. "If it's even possible to destroy it. We don't know how this thing works, let alone how to get rid of it. And what if destroying it has consequences we can't predict?"

Max shifted uncomfortably, glancing at Baxter, who was lying at his feet. "I mean, it's dangerous. We've all seen what it can do. But... it's also powerful. Couldn't we use it to help people? For, you know, practical problems?"

"That's the problem," Theo cut in, his voice sharp. "Using it comes with a cost. Helping one person might hurt someone else. Do you really want that on your conscience?" The room erupted into a flurry of arguments, each voice trying to be heard over the others.

"We could write something small, something harmless," Ellie suggested, her tone pleading. "Test it, see if we can control the outcome better."

"Harmless? Like wishing for happiness?" Theo snapped, his words dripping with sarcasm. "Yeah, that turned out great."

Jake shrugged. "Maybe we're overthinking this. What if we just use it for stuff that doesn't involve people? Like... I don't know, wishing for better weather or more money or something."

"And what happens when the weather turns into a hurricane somewhere else?" Zara countered. "Or the money gets taken from someone who needs it more? We can't assume it works without a trade-off."

Max raised his hands defensively. "Okay, but we can't just destroy it without knowing what we're dealing with. What if it's... I don't know, part of something bigger? What if we need it someday?"

"Need it for what?" Theo shot back. "To ruin more lives?"

Ellie's voice rose above the din, surprising everyone. "Enough!" She rarely raised her voice, and the sudden intensity silenced the room. "We're not going to solve anything by yelling at each other."

The group fell into an uneasy silence, each of them lost in their own thoughts. The notebook seemed to hum with quiet energy, as though aware it was the subject of their deliberation.

Luna hopped onto Ellie's lap, her green eyes fixed on the notebook. Ellie absentmindedly stroked the cat, her mind racing.

Finally, Zara spoke, her voice measured. "We need a plan. Something that doesn't involve jumping to extremes. Destroying it or using it recklessly—neither option feels right."

"Then what?" Jake asked, his playful demeanour replaced by genuine frustration. "We just let it sit there and collect dust?"

Ellie hesitated, then said softly, "What if we try to understand it better? Study it. Figure out where it came from, how it works, and why it does what it does. Maybe then we can make a decision that's... informed."

Before anyone could respond, a collective murmur rippled through the room—a soundless, whispering voice that seemed to come from nowhere and everywhere at once.

"It's not just the notebook."

The group froze, their gazes darting toward their pets, who were suddenly alert. Trixie, Milo, Baxter, and Shadow were all watching them, their expressions unnervingly focused.

"It's connected to you now," the voice continued, layered and shifting, as though each pet were speaking at once.

"What does that mean?" Max asked, his voice trembling.

"You share its magic," the whisper came again. "It's not something you can destroy without destroying part of yourselves."

The weight of the revelation settled over them like a thick fog.

Theo broke the silence, his voice unusually quiet. "So, even if we wanted to destroy it, we couldn't. Not without hurting ourselves."

"And if we keep it, we're stuck with the risk," Zara said grimly.

Jake sighed, rubbing the back of his neck. "Guess that rules out the easy answers."

Ellie looked around at her friends, her heart heavy. "Maybe this isn't about finding an easy answer. Maybe it's about figuring out how to live with it—and each other."

Zara nodded slowly. "We need rules. Boundaries. If we're going to keep it, we must agree on how and when to use it—and when not to."

The group exchanged uneasy glances but nodded in agreement.

They spent the next hour drafting their rules, each suggestion carefully considered and debated.

- **Rule 1:** No wishes without unanimous agreement.
- **Rule 2:** The consequences of any wish must be fully discussed beforehand.
- **Rule 3:** The notebook must remain hidden when not in use.
- **Rule 4:** If a wish affects someone outside the group, they must try to undo it.

When they were done, the rules felt like a fragile shield—better than nothing, but not enough to erase the unease that lingered in the room.

As they left Zara's basement that night, the notebook stayed behind, tucked safely into a locked box. But each of them carried its weight in their hearts, knowing that their connection to it—and to each other—was far from over.

Days turned into weeks, and though life for the group returned to a semblance of normalcy, an unspoken tension hovered over them. The notebook sat locked away in Zara's basement, untouched but never far from anyone's thoughts.
The rules they had established felt more like a fragile truce than a solid foundation. And as the days stretched on, cracks began to show.

Ellie found herself sketching Luna more than usual, her pencil strokes growing restless and jagged. She couldn't shake the memory of the notebook's power—or the temptation it held. There were moments when she'd sit in her room, thinking of how a single wish could erase her worries. The thought felt selfish, but it was always there, like a whisper at the back of her mind.

"Do you think we made the right choice?" Ellie asked Luna one evening.

The cat tilted her head, her emerald eyes reflecting the room's dim light. *"You're asking the wrong question,"* came the soft reply. *"The better question is: Can you trust yourselves?"*

Across town, Max was struggling to focus on his schoolwork. The anxiety that had always been a part of him seemed amplified by the weight of the notebook's presence.

One evening, as he attempted to study for a maths test, he slammed his textbook shut in frustration. "What's the point?" he muttered.

Baxter trotted over, resting his head on Max's lap. For a moment, Max felt a fleeting sense of calm, but it wasn't enough to drown out the spiral of thoughts. What if someone else found out about the notebook? What if they weren't careful enough?

"You're borrowing trouble," came Baxter's quiet voice.

Max frowned. "It's not borrowing trouble if it's already here."

Zara was doing her best to hold the group together, she spent hours pacing her room, Trixie perched on her windowsill like a silent guardian.

"I can't keep doing this," Zara admitted one night. "It's too much. What if I mess up? What if—"

"You will," Trixie interrupted, her voice calm. "And so will they. That's why you have each other."

Zara sighed, running a hand through her hair. "I wish it were that simple."

"It never is," Trixie replied.

Jake, meanwhile, was finding it harder and harder to resist the notebook's allure. The rules they had set felt like chains, stifling the part of him that thrived on action and spontaneity.

"Come on, Milo," he said one afternoon, scooping the ferret into his hoodie pocket. "Let's blow off some steam."

He wandered aimlessly through the park, his thoughts drifting back to the notebook. What if they were overthinking everything? What if he could use it just once, for something small, without telling the others?

"That's a bad idea," Milo's voice chimed in.

Jake smirked. "Since when do I listen to bad ideas?"

Milo chittered, his tone exasperated. "This isn't a joke, Jake. You know what's at stake."

Jake's smile faded. For all his bravado, even he couldn't ignore the weight of those words.

Theo had always been the loner of the group, and the notebook's presence only deepened the gap between him and the others. He kept his distance, convinced that if he stayed detached, he wouldn't be dragged into the chaos.

But Shadow was always by his side, her quiet presence a constant reminder of the connection he couldn't escape.

"You don't have to do this alone," Theo said to her one evening, his voice barely above a whisper.

"Neither do you," Shadow replied.

Theo scoffed, shaking his head. "It's easier that way."

"Easy doesn't mean right," Shadow said, her gaze piercing.

The tension between the group came to a head during a study session at Ellie's house. What started as casual chatter quickly devolved into a heated argument.

"I'm just saying," Jake said, throwing up his hands, "we can't just sit around doing nothing forever."

"And what do you suggest?" Zara snapped. "Using the notebook? Breaking the rules we all agreed on?"

"Maybe!" Jake shot back. "At least it'd be better than pretending everything's fine when it's not."

Ellie stepped in, her voice shaky. "Can we not do this here? My parents are downstairs."

"Maybe we need to do this," Theo said coldly, arms crossed. "If we can't even talk about it without fighting, how are we supposed to handle the notebook?"

The room fell silent, the weight of his words pressing down on them.

It was Luna who broke the silence, her voice echoing softly in Ellie's mind. *"You're stronger together, but only if you choose to be."*

One by one, the other pets chimed in, their whispers threading through the room like a quiet melody.

"Fear will tear you apart."

"Trust each other."

"You've already made it this far."

The group exchanged uneasy glances, the anger and frustration giving way to a shared understanding.

"We need to figure this out," Ellie said finally, her voice steady despite the tremor in her hands. "Together."

Zara nodded, her expression softening. "You're right. We can't let this thing destroy us."

The others murmured their agreement, the bond between them mending.

As they left Ellie's house that evening, the tension between them lingered—but so did the hope that they could face whatever came next, if they stuck together.

Chapter 6 – a Test of leadership

The group had grown quiet since their argument at Ellie's house, the weight of their shared burden pulling them in different directions. The notebook remained locked away, but its presence loomed over them, an unspoken reminder of their dilemma.

Ellie noticed the growing tension among them, the way Zara avoided eye contact, how Theo seemed more withdrawn than usual, and how Jake's jokes had grown sharper, almost defensive. Max was the only one who still tried to bridge the gap, but even his nervous attempts at conversation fell flat.

Sitting in her room one evening, Ellie stared at a blank page in her sketchpad. Luna purred softly at her side, her tail flicking lazily.

"You see it, don't you?" Luna's voice came, soft and soothing.

Ellie nodded. "Yeah. But I don't know how to fix it."

"You don't have to fix everything," Luna said. "Just take the first step."

The next day, Ellie texted everyone, asking them to meet at the old park near the edge of town. It was a place they had spent countless afternoons as kids, long before the notebook had entered their lives.

Zara was the first to arrive, her expression guarded. "What's this about?"

"You'll see," Ellie said with a small smile.

Jake showed up next, Milo poking his head out of Jake's hoodie pocket. "This better not be another intervention," he joked, though there was a hint of unease in his voice.

Theo and Max arrived together, Shadow and Baxter trotting alongside them. Theo's usual sarcasm was replaced by a wary silence, while Max looked relieved to see the others.

Ellie took a deep breath, her heart pounding. She wasn't used to taking charge, but she knew this moment mattered.

"I asked you all to come here because... well, we need to talk," Ellie began.

Jake raised an eyebrow. "About the notebook, I'm guessing?"

Ellie nodded. "Yeah, but not just the notebook. About us. We've been falling apart lately, and I think it's because we're all scared."

Theo scoffed. "Scared of what? The magical death trap we keep locked in a box?"

"Scared of what it means," Ellie said firmly, surprising even herself with the steadiness in her voice. "It's not just the notebook. It's what it's done to us—and what it could do if we're not careful."

Zara crossed her arms. "And what do you suggest we do about it?"

Ellie hesitated, then looked around at her friends. "We need to stop thinking of it as just a problem to solve. It's part of our lives now, whether we like it or not. And if we're going to

handle it, we must trust each other again."

The others exchanged uncertain glances, but Ellie pressed on.

"Look, I know it's not easy. I'm not saying we must be perfect,

but we can't keep avoiding each other or pretending this isn't

happening." She paused, her hands trembling slightly. "We're

stronger together. We've already proven that."

Max spoke up, his voice tentative. "So, what do we do?"

Ellie smiled, the corners of her lips twitching with nerves. "We

start small. No more hiding how we feel, no more shutting

each other out. And maybe... maybe we take the notebook out

again. Not to use it, just to face it together."

The suggestion hung in the air, heavy and uncertain.

Zara was the first to nod. "Alright. But only if we all agree."

Theo rolled his eyes but muttered, "Fine. I'm in."

Jake grinned. "Guess I can't let you all have the fun without

me."

Max nodded quickly. "Yeah, me too."

Ellie felt a surge of relief. "Okay. Tomorrow, Zara's basement. Let's face it together."

As they left the park that evening, Ellie felt a newfound sense of purpose. She still didn't have all the answers, but for the first time, she felt like she was leading—not because she wanted to, but because her friends needed her to.

Chapter 7 – a Family secret

The next morning, Ellie was gathering her things to head to Zara's house when her mom called her downstairs.

"Ellie, can I talk to you for a second?" her mom asked, leaning against the kitchen counter. There was a strange tone in her voice—serious but tinged with hesitation.

"Sure," Ellie said, setting her bag down. "What's up?"

Her mom glanced out the window, as if searching for the right words. "I have something that... I think you need to see."

Ellie's stomach tightened. Her mom wasn't usually one for dramatics, which made the moment more unsettling. "What is it?"

Her mom reached into a drawer and pulled out a worn leather-bound book. It wasn't the notebook—but it looked eerily similar.

"This belonged to your grandmother," her mom explained, setting the book on the table. "She always said it was special, but I never really believed her. I thought it was just one of her stories. But now... I'm not so sure."

Ellie's fingers hovered over the cover. It was scuffed and faded, but the resemblance to their notebook was undeniable. "Why are you showing me this now?"

Her mom hesitated. "Because I think it might be connected to... whatever's been going on with you lately. I know you've been distracted, Ellie. Distant. And I can't help but feel like this might explain some things."

Ellie opened the journal carefully, her heart pounding. The first few pages were filled with delicate handwriting—her grandmother's, she realised.

The entries started innocuously enough, describing day-to-day life on the farm where her grandmother had grown up. But as Ellie flipped further, the tone shifted.

"March 14th, 1953. I wrote something today, and it came true. I didn't mean for it to happen, but it did. The words are alive somehow, and they don't come without a price."

Ellie's breath caught. She skimmed ahead, her grandmother's words growing more frantic.

"April 2nd, 1953. I thought I could control it, but I was wrong. The notebook has its own will, its own rules. I can't keep this secret much longer."

Ellie flipped to the final entry, her grandmother's handwriting shaky and uneven.

"May 17th, 1953. I've hidden it away. It's too dangerous to keep using, but I can't destroy it. The magic is older than I am—older than any of us. If you're reading this, whoever you are, be careful. It has a way of finding its way back."

Ellie's stomach churned. Could her grandmother have been talking about the notebook? Was it the same one?

Her mom placed a hand on her shoulder. "Ellie, if there's something you're not telling me, you need to be honest."

Ellie hesitated. She wanted to tell her mom everything, to unload the weight of the secret she'd been carrying. But how could she explain the notebook without sounding crazy?

"I'll be careful," she said finally.

Her mom didn't look convinced but nodded. "Alright. Just… promise me you'll talk to me if you need to. Whatever's going on, you don't have to face it alone."

As Ellie walked to Zara's house, the journal felt heavy in her bag. She couldn't stop replaying her grandmother's words in her mind.

When she arrived, the others were already waiting.

"You're late," Zara said, though her tone was more curious than annoyed.

"Sorry," Ellie said, pulling out the journal. "I think I found something we need to talk about."

She explained everything—her grandmother's entries, the warnings, and the possibility that their notebook had a history they didn't understand.

The room fell silent as the weight of her revelation sank in.

"So, what does this mean?" Max asked nervously.

"It means we're not the first ones to deal with this," Ellie said.

"And if my grandmother couldn't control it, we need to be even more careful."

Theo leaned back, his expression unreadable. "Great. So now it's a family curse."

"It's not a curse," Ellie said, her voice steady. "But it's definitely not random, either."

The group exchanged uneasy glances, the tension between them renewed. The notebook's secrets were deeper than any of them had imagined, and Ellie could feel the weight of her grandmother's warning pressing down on her.

For the first time, she truly understood the responsibility they were facing—and the danger that came with it.

The notebook's weight pressed heavily on Ellie's thoughts as the group gathered in Zara's basement. The journal sat in the centre of the table, its leather cover worn and weathered, a stark reminder of the dangers they faced.

"We need a plan," Ellie said, breaking the silence. Her voice was firm, though her heart raced.

Zara leaned forward, her analytical mind already ticking. "Agreed. If your grandmother couldn't control it, we need to be smarter than she was. We need to set more rules."

Theo smirked. "Oh, sure. Rules will stop a magical notebook from messing with us."

"Better than nothing," Zara shot back. "Do you have a better idea?"

Theo shrugged, leaning back in his chair. "Not yet."

Jake, flipping a coin between his fingers, chimed in. "We could always bury it and pretend it doesn't exist."

Max shook his head, his glasses sliding down his nose. "We tried ignoring it before, and it didn't work. The notebook... it feels like it's waiting for us to do something. Like it's alive."

Zara leaned back, tapping her pen against the notebook. "How could we protect ourselves if something goes wrong?"

Ellie considered this, flipping through her grandmother's journal again. "She mentioned hiding it when it became too dangerous. Maybe we can find a way to contain it, like a box or something."

"A magical lock?" Jake suggested with a grin.

"Not everything has to be magic," Zara replied. "What about a safe with a combination only we know?"

Theo frowned. "What happens if it... I don't know, tries to escape? We've already seen how it seems to act on its own."

Ellie nodded thoughtfully. "We'll need a backup plan. Something to destroy it, if it comes to that."

The room fell silent at the suggestion. Destroying the notebook felt extreme, but they all knew it might come to that someday.

"I'll look into it," Zara said quietly. "Maybe there's a way to counteract whatever magic it has."

As the meeting went on, the group began to feel a flicker of their old connection. For the first time in weeks, they were working together, their focus on a common goal.

Jake started cracking jokes again, lightening the mood even as they discussed worst-case scenarios. Theo's sarcasm softened, and he offered genuine suggestions. Max seemed less nervous, his hands steady as he wrote down their plans. Ellie watched them, a quiet sense of pride swelling in her chest. They were scared, yes, but they were facing their fear together.

As they wrapped up, Zara handed Ellie the list of rules. "You're the one holding us together," she said, her voice matter of fact. "You should keep this."

Ellie took the paper, her fingers brushing against Zara's for a moment. "Thanks. But this isn't just on me. We're in this together."

Zara nodded. "Always."

That night, Ellie sat in her room, the rules pinned to her corkboard and the journal on her desk. Luna curled up beside her, her tail flicking against Ellie's arm.

"You're doing well," Luna said softly.

Ellie smiled, stroking her cat's fur. "We'll see."

As she gazed at the notebook's faint outline in her bag, she felt a renewed sense of determination. The challenges ahead were daunting, but they were ready. They had rules, a plan, and each other.

For the first time since the notebook entered their lives, Ellie felt prepared.

The group reconvened the next afternoon at Theo's house. His garage was cluttered with tools, old furniture, and the faint smell of oil. It was the perfect place for their experiment— remote, private, and quiet.

Ellie set the notebook on a cleared workbench, the others gathering around her. "We've talked about containing it," she began, "and I think we should use the notebook itself to secure it. If we're careful, it might be the best way."

Max adjusted his glasses nervously. "You want us to... wish it locked away?"

"Yes," Ellie said. "But we'll word it carefully to avoid any unintended consequences."

Zara nodded, folding her arms. "It's risky, but it makes sense. A magic problem needs a magic solution."

Jake grinned. "Finally, we're doing something cool with it again. No offense to all the rule-writing."

Theo raised an eyebrow. "This could backfire spectacularly. You all realise that, right?"

Ellie met his gaze, steady and calm. "That's why we're doing this together. If something goes wrong, we'll handle it— together."

The group spent an hour debating the exact wording. Every suggestion was scrutinised, dissected, and rephrased.

"What if it traps us instead?" Max asked, biting his lip.

"Then we don't phrase it like a trap," Zara replied. "We need to be specific. The notebook gets secured, but it doesn't harm or affect anyone in the process."

Jake grabbed a scrap of paper and began doodling a box.

"What if the lock only opens when all five of us are present? Like a fingerprint thing, but... you know, magic."

"I like that," Ellie said. "It ensures no one can use it alone."

They settled on the final wording:

"I wish for the notebook to be secured inside a wooden box, locked in a way that only the five of us together can open it, with no harm or unintended consequences to anyone."

Max read it aloud one last time, his voice trembling slightly. "Are we sure about this?"

Ellie placed a reassuring hand on his shoulder. "As sure as we can be."

Ellie took the pen, her hand steady despite the butterflies in her stomach. She opened the notebook and carefully wrote the wish, each letter deliberate.

As she finished the last word, the notebook began to glow faintly, a golden light emanating from its pages. The air in the garage grew warmer, tingling with an electric charge.

Then, with a low hum, the notebook lifted off the table, spinning slowly. Wood began to materialise around it, twisting and shaping itself into a box. Intricate carvings adorned its surface, depicting animals, symbols, and patterns that seemed to shift when viewed from different angles.

The box landed gently on the workbench, the notebook sealed inside. A lock appeared on the front, its mechanism glowing faintly before dimming.

The group stared in awe.

"That was... intense," Jake said, breaking the silence.

"It worked," Zara said, her voice filled with a mix of relief and wonder.

Theo approached the box cautiously, running his fingers over the carvings. "It's warm."

Ellie stepped forward. "Let's test it."

Each of them placed a hand on the box, their fingers overlapping. For a moment, nothing happened. Then, the lock clicked, and the lid creaked open, revealing the notebook nestled inside.

When they closed the lid, the box sealed itself again with a soft click.

"Perfect," Ellie said, smiling for the first time in what felt like days.

Max exhaled deeply. "I can't believe that actually worked."

Jake leaned against the workbench, grinning. "Admit it, Theo— you thought it was going to blow up."

Theo rolled his eyes but smirked. "I still think it might, someday."

The box was placed in a safe spot in Zara's loft, hidden beneath blankets and old storage bins. For the first time since the notebook had come into their lives, the group felt a semblance of control.

"We did it," Ellie said as they stood together, looking at the sealed box. "Now we can take a step back and breathe."

"Until the next crisis," Theo muttered, but his tone lacked its usual edge.

Jake clapped him on the back. "Hey, let's enjoy the victory while it lasts."

As they left Zara's house, Ellie felt a sense of relief wash over her. They weren't rid of the notebook, but they'd taken a step toward managing its power.

For now, that was enough.

Chapter 8 – The calm before the storm

For the first time in weeks, Ellie felt a sense of normalcy as she walked home from school. The crisp air carried the faint scent of rain, and the world seemed quieter somehow. The notebook, now secured in its intricately carved wooden box, hadn't crossed her mind all day—until now.

As she rounded the corner to her street, Luna darted out from the bushes, her silver fur catching the fading sunlight.

"You're late," Luna said, her tone playful.

Ellie knelt to scratch behind Luna's ears, smiling faintly.

"You're starting to sound like Zara."

"Someone has to keep you on your toes."

The days that followed were oddly peaceful. With the notebook locked away, the group tried to reclaim their routines. Zara buried herself in homework and extracurriculars, while Theo spent more time sketching in his notebook. Max, relieved to have some distance from the chaos, started volunteering at the local library.

Jake, true to form, had thrown himself into another harebrained scheme, this time involving an attempt to train his dog, Scout, to skateboard.

Ellie watched as Jake ran alongside Scout, holding the leash and cheering. Scout, a wiry mutt with endless energy, seemed more interested in chasing a butterfly than staying on the board.

"You're going to break something," Ellie called, laughing.

Jake grinned, his hair sticking up wildly. "Only if I'm lucky! You should try it with Luna."

Ellie shook her head, still smiling. "She'd shred the board—and probably me."

Despite the surface calm, Ellie couldn't shake the feeling that something was off. The connection the group had felt during their shared burden with the notebook was fading. Without the constant threat of its power, they seemed to drift apart. At their last meeting, Theo had been quieter than usual, Zara had seemed distracted, and Max hadn't stayed long. Even Jake's jokes felt more forced than before. The group had agreed that Ellie should keep the notebook at her house.

Sitting in her room one evening, Ellie stared at the sealed box on her desk. The carvings shimmered faintly in the dim light, as though alive.

"Do you think we made the right choice?" she asked Luna, who was perched on the windowsill.

The cat flicked her tail thoughtfully. "You made the best choice you could with the information you had. That's all anyone can do."

"But what if it's not enough?"

Luna didn't answer, but her golden eyes seemed to hold a quiet understanding.

Rain began to fall the next morning, a steady drizzle that quickly grew into a downpour. Ellie arrived at school soaked despite her umbrella, her auburn hair sticking to her face.

The others were already at their usual table in the library. Zara was hunched over a textbook, Jake was doodling on the back of a worksheet, and Max was fiddling with his pen. Theo leaned against the window, staring out at the rain.

Ellie slid into a chair and set her bag down. "Hey."

"Hey," Jake said, tossing her a grin. "Wet enough for you out there?"

"Like swimming to class," Ellie replied.

They lapsed into silence, the sound of rain pattering against the windows filling the space.

Zara finally looked up, her eyes scanning the group. "We've been quiet lately."

Max nodded, but didn't say anything.

"It's weird, isn't it?" Jake said, breaking the tension. "Not having the notebook hanging over us. Feels... empty."

Theo snorted. "Empty is better than cursed."

"Is it, though?" Jake asked, his voice uncharacteristically serious. "We're not *us* without it. Not really."

Ellie frowned. "That's not true. The notebook doesn't define us."

"Doesn't it?" Jake shot back. "Without it, we're just... people who sit at the same table."

"That's not fair," Zara said, her tone sharp. "We're more than that. We've been through too much to let it tear us apart now."

As the conversation died down, Ellie glanced out the window, her stomach twisting. The rain seemed heavier than it should have been, the drops pounding against the glass with an almost unnatural force.

Something was coming.

She could feel it in her bones.

"Let's meet at my place this weekend," Ellie said suddenly.

"We can hang out. No notebook talk. Just us."

The others exchanged glances before nodding.

"Fine by me," Jake said, flashing a grin. "As long as there's food."

Zara smirked. "There's always food."

Ellie smiled, but the unease in her chest remained.

As they packed up and left for class, the rain continued to fall, relentless and unyielding.

Ellie had spent most of Saturday preparing for the group's arrival. Her room was tidied, snacks were arranged on the coffee table, and Luna had been bribed with an extra helping of tuna to behave herself. The box with the notebook sat untouched on her desk, its carved surface glinting faintly in the evening light.

By the time the doorbell rang, the smell of popcorn filled the house, and Ellie felt a small sense of relief. Tonight wasn't about the notebook. It was about reconnecting, trying to rediscover the bond that had brought them together in the first place.

"Coming!" she called, heading downstairs.

When she opened the door, Jake was standing there, holding a bag of assorted candy and grinning like he'd just won a prize.

"Ellie! Your hero has arrived." He pushed past her dramatically, plopping the bag on the counter.

Ellie rolled her eyes but smiled. "You're the first one here. Try not to eat everything before the others arrive."

"No promises." Jake was already rummaging through the bag.

Soon after, the rest of the group trickled in. Zara carried a tray of homemade brownies, Max brought a stack of board games, and Theo showed up empty-handed but with a sarcastic quip about contributing his "incredible presence."

Ellie's living room filled with the sound of laughter and chatter as they settled in. Luna made her rounds, inspecting each of them in turn before curling up on the armrest of Ellie's chair.

"So," Jake said, balancing a piece of brownie on his nose like a circus act, "what's the plan for tonight? Truth or dare? Secret confessions? A séance?"

Theo rolled his eyes. "We're not twelve, Jake."

"Speak for yourself," Jake shot back, the brownie toppling into his lap.

Ellie smirked. "I was thinking board games, maybe a movie later. Something low-key."

"Low-key is good," Max said, adjusting his glasses. "Low-key is... safe."

Jake nudged him playfully. "You're such a buzzkill, Max."

They started with a game of *Codenames*, quickly devolving into bickering as Jake insisted on giving the most obscure clues imaginable.

134

"'Dragon'? Really?" Zara said, raising an eyebrow. "What does that have to do with anything on this board?"

"It's obvious!" Jake said defensively.

"It's *not*," Theo muttered, scribbling sarcastic commentary on a scrap of paper while the others argued.

Despite the chaos, the laughter was genuine. Ellie found herself relaxing for the first time in weeks.

By the time they moved on to *Uno*, Jake had somehow acquired a stack of nearly every Wild card in the deck and was cackling like a cartoon villain as he unleashed them one by one.

"You're the worst," Zara groaned as Jake slapped down another +4.

"Admit it, you love it," Jake said with a wink.

As the night wore on, the games gave way to quieter conversations. The group sprawled across the living room, the buzz of earlier excitement settling into something softer.

Ellie sat cross-legged on the floor, leaning against the couch. Luna had claimed her lap, purring contentedly. Across the room, Max was trying to explain the rules of chess to Theo, who seemed more interested in mocking Max's enthusiasm than learning.

"I don't get it," Theo said, staring at the board. "Why not just flip the table and declare victory?"

"Because that's not how chess works," Max said, exasperated.

"It's how *my* chess works."

Ellie laughed, glancing over at Zara and Jake, who were sitting by the coffee table. Zara was sketching something in a notebook—not *the* notebook, just an ordinary one—and Jake was tossing gummy bears into his mouth, missing half of them.

"Do you think we'll ever... go back to normal?" Zara asked suddenly, her voice low.

Jake shrugged, tossing another gummy bear into the air.

"What's normal, anyway? I don't think we were ever normal to begin with."

Zara smiled faintly but didn't respond.

Ellie felt a pang in her chest as she watched them. She couldn't help but think about how much had changed since the notebook had entered their lives. They were different now closer in some ways, fractured in others.

"Earth to Ellie," Jake said, snapping his fingers in front of her face.

She blinked, startled. "What?"

"You spaced out," he said, grinning. "Were you dreaming about my epic Uno victory?"

Ellie rolled her eyes. "Hardly."

"Good," Theo said dryly. "No one needs to relive that nightmare."

As midnight approached, the energy in the room shifted again. The group moved closer together, huddling around the coffee table as Jake suggested telling ghost stories.

"Ghost stories?" Max asked, his voice tinged with nervousness.

"Don't worry, Max," Jake teased. "I'll hold your hand if you get scared."

"Hard pass."

They took turns telling increasingly ridiculous stories, each trying to outdo the last. By the time Theo finished his tale about a haunted vending machine that dispensed cursed snacks, they were all laughing so hard they could barely breathe.

For a moment, it felt like nothing had changed.

But as the laughter faded and the clock ticked closer to one, Ellie couldn't shake the feeling that the calm wouldn't last.

The days following their gathering brought an uneasy quiet. The laughter and camaraderie of that night lingered in Ellie's memory, but so did the weight of unspoken thoughts. The notebook remained locked away, but its presence was palpable—a question mark hovering over them all.

Ellie found herself sitting at her desk one evening, staring at the carved box. Luna was curled up on her bed, watching her with half-lidded eyes.

"You're thinking about it again," the cat said softly, her voice almost a purr.

Ellie sighed. "Aren't you?"

Luna stretched, her tail flicking lazily. "I think it's dangerous. But I'm a cat. We're naturally suspicious."

The next time the group met, they couldn't avoid the subject any longer. It was Zara who brought it up, her tone steady but tinged with reluctance.

"We need to talk about the notebook," she said, glancing around the circle.

They were at Max's house this time, crammed into his small living room. The rain outside made the space feel smaller, the walls pressing in.

"What about it?" Theo asked, arms crossed. "We locked it up. End of story."

"It's not that simple," Zara replied. "We agreed to give it more thought. And I've been thinking... what if we're wasting an opportunity?"

Jake perked up. "Finally, someone gets it! We've got this thing that can literally make anything happen, and we're just letting it gather dust."

"Because it's dangerous," Max said quickly. "You saw what happened last time. We can't control it."

"But what if we could?" Zara countered. "What if we set rules, used it carefully?"

Theo scoffed. "Carefully? That's not how it works. You can't make a wish without paying the price."

"What would you wish for, then?" Ellie asked, her voice cutting through the growing tension.

The room fell silent.

Jake leaned back, a thoughtful expression replacing his usual grin. "I don't know. Maybe... a way to make people laugh, like, really laugh. No sadness. No strings attached."

"You know there'd be strings," Theo said.

Jake shrugged. "Yeah, but still. Imagine how cool that'd be."

Zara spoke next, her tone hesitant. "I think... I'd wish for more time. Time to fix things, to get everything right."

"Time comes at a cost," Theo said quietly. "What if it's someone else's time you're taking?"

Zara didn't respond, but her jaw tightened.

Max fidgeted with the hem of his sweater. "I'd wish to be brave," he admitted. "To not feel scared all the time."

"That's not a bad wish," Ellie said gently.

"But what if someone else ended up more scared because of it?" Theo asked, his gaze steady.

"What about you?" Zara asked, turning to Ellie.

Ellie hesitated. She hadn't allowed herself to think about it, not fully. But now that the question was out in the open, it was impossible to ignore.

"I don't know," she admitted. "Maybe... maybe to understand what we're supposed to do. To know if we're making the right choices."

Theo raised an eyebrow. "And if someone else ended up more lost because of your wish?"

Ellie looked down at her hands. "That's why I haven't made it."

"And you?" Zara asked Theo.

He smirked, but it lacked his usual sharpness. "I wouldn't waste my time."

"That's a lie," Jake said, pointing a gummy bear at him. "Come on, Theo. Spill."

Theo's expression hardened. "Fine. I'd wish for people to stop being so fake. To stop pretending they care when they don't."

The room went quiet.

"That's... heavy," Jake said, his voice uncharacteristically soft.

Theo shrugged, avoiding their eyes. "Doesn't matter. I'm not making the wish."

The discussion spiralled from there, each of them throwing out hypothetical wishes, debating their consequences. Jake argued for the potential good they could do, while Max insisted the risks were too great. Zara tried to mediate, but her own doubts began to seep through.

Ellie stayed mostly quiet, listening as the tension in the room grew. The longer they talked, the clearer it became that the notebook was more than a tool—it was a temptation, a test of their values and their limits.

Finally, she stood. "Enough."

The group fell silent, turning to her.

"This isn't getting us anywhere," Ellie said firmly. "We locked the notebook away for a reason. Until we can figure out how to use it without hurting anyone, we don't touch it."

"But what if we never figure it out?" Jake asked.

"Then maybe we don't deserve to," Ellie replied.

The group dispersed not long after, the tension still hanging in the air.

Ellie walked home in the rain, her thoughts churning. She didn't have all the answers, none of them did. But she knew one thing for certain: the notebook had already changed them. Whether for better or worse remained to be seen.

Chapter 9 – a Whisper in the dark

The rain tapped gently against Ellie's bedroom window, a rhythmic pattern that would have been soothing on any other night. But tonight, the sound seemed to magnify the unease that had settled over her since the group's heated discussion. The carved wooden box sat on her desk, illuminated by the dim light of her desk lamp. Luna lay curled up on her pillow, her ears twitching in her sleep. Ellie couldn't stop staring at the box, as if it might spring open on its own.

She hadn't opened it since they sealed the notebook away. The thought of the notebook's power still sent a shiver down her spine.

Maybe we don't deserve to use it. The words she had spoken to the group echoed in her mind. She believed them. Didn't she?

The room seemed quieter than usual, as if the rain outside had muffled all other sounds. Ellie tried to focus on the sketchpad in her lap, her pencil moving across the page in slow, deliberate strokes. She wasn't drawing anything in particular—just shapes, lines, patterns.

Then, just as she was beginning to relax, she heard it.

A voice.

Faint and distant, like a whisper carried on the wind.

She froze, her pencil hovering above the page. Her eyes darted to Luna, but the cat was still asleep, her tail twitching lazily.

"Ellie..."

The voice was clearer now, low and melodic, yet impossible to place. It wasn't coming from outside. It was inside the room.

"Who's there?" Ellie asked, her voice barely above a whisper.

There was no response, but the air in the room felt heavier, charged with an energy she couldn't explain.

Ellie's gaze shifted to the box. Her heart began to race as she noticed something she hadn't seen before: the faintest shimmer of light seeping through the edges of the lid.

"Ellie..." the voice came again, this time more insistent.

She stood, her legs trembling, and took a hesitant step toward the desk. The air around the box seemed to hum, a low vibration that she could feel in her chest.

Luna stirred, lifting her head and letting out a low, warning growl. The sound snapped Ellie out of her trance, and she stumbled back, her breathing ragged.

The light around the box flickered and then vanished, leaving the room in silence once more.

Ellie sat down on her bed, her hands trembling as she clutched her sketchpad. Luna leapt down and nuzzled her leg, her fur bristling.

"It spoke to me," Ellie whispered, more to herself than to the cat.

Luna's green eyes narrowed. *"The notebook?"*

Ellie nodded.

"That's not good."

"No kidding," Ellie muttered, running a hand through her hair.

"It's testing you," Luna said, her voice unusually serious.

"Seeing how far you'll go. You need to tell the others."

Ellie hesitated. "What if they think I'm imagining it? Or worse—what if it happens to them too?"

"Better they know. A secret like this only makes it stronger."

The rest of the night passed in a haze. Ellie didn't dare close her eyes, afraid that the voice would return the moment she let her guard down.

By morning, the rain had stopped, and the sunlight streaming through her window felt like a lifeline. But the unease lingered, a dark cloud that refused to lift.

She knew what she had to do.

Ellie gathered the group later that day, insisting they meet at her house.

As they filed into her room, the tension was palpable. Jake flopped onto her bed, Zara leaned against the wall with her arms crossed, and Max sat on the edge of her desk chair, fidgeting nervously. Theo lingered near the door, his expression unreadable.

"This better be good," Theo said. "I had plans, you know."

Ellie ignored him, her eyes on the box. "Something happened last night. I think... I think the notebook tried to talk to me."

Jake sat up, his playful demeanour vanishing. "Wait, what?"

"It called my name," Ellie said, her voice steady despite the fear bubbling beneath the surface. "And the box... it started glowing."

"That's... not normal," Max said, his voice shaky.

"No kidding," Zara said, her brow furrowed. "Did you try to open it?"

Ellie shook her head. "No. But it felt like it wanted me to."

The room fell silent as the weight of Ellie's words sank in.

"So, what do we do?" Jake asked finally.

"We stick to the plan," Zara said firmly. "The box stays sealed. No one touches it."

"But what if it doesn't stop?" Max asked, his voice barely above a whisper.

Theo's eyes narrowed. "Then maybe the problem isn't the notebook. Maybe it's us."

Ellie looked at him, confused. "What do you mean?"

Theo shrugged. "It's feeding off something—our doubts, our curiosity, whatever. If we keep obsessing over it, it's just going to get worse."

The group spent the next hour debating their next steps, but

no clear answers emerged. When they finally left, the air

between them felt heavier than ever.

Ellie sat alone in her room, staring at the box once more. She

knew Theo was right—the notebook was feeding off them,

pushing them closer to the edge.

But knowing that didn't make it any easier to resist.

Chapter 10 – The unseen threat

The days after Ellie's revelation passed in a haze of unease. The group had agreed to keep the notebook locked away, but an unspoken fear gnawed at each of them. Something had shifted—subtly, yet undeniably.

Ellie couldn't shake the feeling that they were being watched. At first, she dismissed it as paranoia, but the sense of unease grew stronger with each passing day. Luna seemed more on edge, too, her ears constantly swivelling toward sounds that Ellie couldn't hear.

It started small. Zara noticed her alarm clock blinking at odd hours, even though she hadn't touched it. Jake swore he heard footsteps behind him while skateboarding home one evening, but when he turned around, the street was empty.

Max found himself waking up in the middle of the night, drenched in sweat, his dreams a blur of unsettling images he couldn't quite remember.

Theo, ever the sceptic, dismissed their concerns. "You're all just stressed out. We've been through a lot. It's messing with your heads."

But even Theo couldn't explain why the streetlight outside his bedroom window flickered every time he tried to sleep.

One evening, Ellie was sketching in her room when Luna suddenly jumped onto her desk, knocking over a cup of pencils.

"Luna!" Ellie exclaimed, but the cat didn't respond. Instead, she stared at the window, her fur bristling.

Ellie followed her gaze but saw nothing unusual. The backyard was quiet, bathed in the golden light of the setting sun.

"What is it?" Ellie asked softly, but Luna didn't move.

"Something's out there," the cat finally said, her voice low and tense.

Ellie's stomach tightened. "What do you mean? What kind of something?"

Luna didn't answer. Instead, she leapt off the desk and slinked toward the window, her tail flicking with agitation.

Ellie stood and peered outside, her eyes scanning the yard for any sign of movement. She saw nothing.

But she felt it.

A presence.

The group convened the next day at Zara's house. The atmosphere was tense, each of them carrying the weight of their own strange experiences.

Ellie recounted what had happened with Luna, her voice steady but tinged with unease.

"I think... something's watching us," she said.

Jake frowned. "Like, what? A ghost?"

"Or something worse," Max muttered, his voice barely audible.

"There's no such thing as ghosts," Theo said, though his tone lacked conviction. "Whatever's happening, it's just... coincidence. Weird stuff happens all the time."

"Not like this," Zara said firmly. "This is different. And you know it."

As they talked, an idea began to take shape—a terrifying possibility they couldn't ignore.

"What if it's the notebook?" Max asked.

"What about it?" Jake replied.

"What if... it's not just a thing? What if it's... alive?"

The room fell silent.

"That's ridiculous," Theo said, but there was a hint of uncertainty in his voice.

"Is it?" Ellie asked. "It spoke to me, Theo. It tried to make me try to open the box. What if it's more than just a book?"

"And what if it's connected to everything that's been happening?" Zara added. "The strange dreams, the footsteps, the... presence. What if it's testing us?"

The idea hung in the air, unspoken but undeniable. The notebook wasn't just an object—it was a force, one that seemed to grow stronger the more they engaged with it.

"We need to figure out what we're dealing with," Ellie said finally. "And fast. Before it gets worse."

"How?" Jake asked.

"We start by gathering information," Zara said. "We look for patterns, clues. Anything that might help us understand what's going on."

"And then what?" Theo asked.

"Then we figure out how to stop it," Ellie said, her voice firm. For the first time, she felt the full weight of her role as the group's leader. It wasn't just about keeping them together—it was about protecting them.

156

Whatever the notebook was, it wasn't going to make that easy.

The next few days were spent scouring every resource they could think of. Libraries, internet forums, old books from lofts—they left no stone unturned. The group divided their efforts, each taking a different angle to uncover the truth about the notebook.

Ellie, Zara, Max, Jake, and Theo reconvened in Zara's garage, a dimly lit but spacious room that had become their unofficial headquarters. The air smelled faintly of motor oil, and the sound of a dripping faucet echoed in the background.

"We've got to connect the dots," Ellie said, spreading her notes across the table. "If we're going to figure out what this thing is, we need to share everything we've found."

Ellie was the first to speak. "I started looking through my old sketches to see if I'd ever drawn anything... unusual." She hesitated, glancing at the others. "And I found this."

She placed a page on the table. It was an intricate sketch of a tree, its roots twisting and curling like veins. Hidden among the roots was a symbol—a spiral encased in a triangle.

"That's weird," Jake said, leaning in for a closer look. "You think it means something?"

"I don't know," Ellie admitted. "But I don't remember drawing that part. It's like... it just appeared."

Zara had taken a more methodical approach, spending hours in the local library. She spread several photocopied pages across the table.

"These are stories I found about objects with similar properties—things that grant wishes but come with consequences." She pointed to one article about a cursed mirror. "In every case, the object seemed to feed off the user's emotions, growing stronger the more it was used."

"So, it's like a parasite," Max said, his voice trembling.

"Exactly," Zara said. "The more we interact with it, the more power it has over us."

Max, true to his tech-savvy nature, had combed through countless internet forums and chat rooms.

"I found this," he said, pulling up a thread on his laptop. The title read: *'Cursed Objects and Their Effects.'*

The group leaned in as Max scrolled through the posts. One caught their attention: 'I found an old book that could grant wishes, but it destroyed my family. Be careful what you wish for.'

"That sounds eerily familiar," Jake muttered.

Max nodded. "A lot of these stories end the same way—people get greedy, the object twists their wishes, and things spiral out of control."

Jake had spent his time observing the group's pets. "Okay, this might sound crazy, but... I think the animals know something."

"Like what?" Theo asked, sceptical.

"Like, they can sense the notebook's energy," Jake said. "Luna's been acting weird, right, Ellie? And my dog, Shadow, started growling at the box when I brought it near him."

Ellie nodded. "Luna's definitely been on edge."

"Animals are more sensitive to stuff like this," Jake said. "Maybe they can help us figure out what we're dealing with."

Theo, ever the pragmatist, had spent his time analysing the group's behaviour.

"Look, I'm not saying the notebook isn't dangerous," he began, "but I think we need to consider how much of this is just... us. Our fears, our doubts. If it's feeding off our emotions, then maybe the best way to fight it is to stop letting it control us."

"That's easier said than done," Zara said.

"Yeah, but it's worth a shot," Theo replied. "If we stay calm and stick to the facts, maybe we can weaken its hold on us."

As the group pieced together their findings, a pattern began to emerge. The notebook wasn't just a tool—it was a sentient force, one that thrived on their emotions and interactions.

"It's like it's playing a game with us," Ellie said. "It wants us to keep using it, to keep feeding it."

"So, what do we do?" Jake asked.

"We keep it locked away," Zara said firmly. "And we stop engaging with it—no more talking about it, no more thinking about it. At least for now."

"And if that doesn't work?" Max asked.

"Then we'll find another way," Ellie said, her voice steady.

The group nodded, their resolve strengthened by the shared knowledge. But as they left Zara's garage that evening, each of them felt the weight of the unseen threat still looming over them.

Chapter 11 – Cracks in the surface

The group had agreed to put the notebook out of their minds, to forget it for a while and focus on their normal lives. For the first few days, it seemed like they were succeeding. They spent time together, laughed, and even enjoyed moments of peace, something that felt elusive in the wake of their discovery. But the cracks began to form, invisible at first, then slowly growing wider until they were undeniable.

Ellie spent most of her days in the studio, sketching as she usually did. But now, her hand moved with an odd sense of urgency, as if the pencil itself was trying to escape her grasp. Her thoughts wandered, often drifting back to the box in her room, to the whispering voice that had spoken to her. She tried to focus on the work in front of her, but the sketchpad felt heavy—an anchor pulling her back toward something she couldn't shake.

It was as if the notebook was still with her, even though it was locked away. The weight of it was there, in every stroke of her pencil, in every breath she took. Luna, her ever-watchful cat, kept her distance, sensing something Ellie couldn't name. "Maybe it's just stress," Ellie muttered to herself. But deep down, she knew it wasn't. It was more than that.

Zara had always been the rock of their group, the one who held it all together. But now, she felt the pressure mounting, more than ever. She couldn't shake the feeling that something was wrong, that the calm they'd found was fragile and temporary.

At school, she found herself snapping at people for no reason. She was irritable, distracted, and unable to focus on anything other than the notebook.

It wasn't like her. Zara was always in control. But now, every decision felt weighed down by doubt. She couldn't look at the others without wondering if they were feeling the same thing. Was it her, or was it something else?

And what if they were wrong? What if, by not addressing the notebook, they had given it the power to slip into the cracks of their lives, silently influencing them all?

Max's anxiety, which had always been a part of him, was worse than ever. He had trouble sleeping at night, haunted by dreams he couldn't remember but knew were tied to the notebook. His days were filled with restlessness, and every time he looked at the clock, time seemed to slip away too quickly, as if the world around him was moving faster than he could keep up.

Every sound seemed amplified: footsteps in the hallway, whispers in the corners of his mind. He felt like he was being watched—always.

"I need to take a break from all of this," Max said to the group one afternoon as they gathered in Zara's garage. "I can't keep going like this."

"What do you mean?" Jake asked, not quite understanding.

Max rubbed his temples. "It's not just the notebook. It's... everything. It feels like I'm losing control."

"I think we all are," Ellie said softly, glancing at Luna, who was perched on the windowsill, watching them intently.

Jake, ever the wild card, seemed unaffected on the surface. He joked, he laughed, and he did his best to distract the group from the growing tension. But even he couldn't escape the subtle pull of the notebook.

The world around him started to feel... off. Little things, like the way shadows seemed to stretch too far, or how his thoughts would blur for a second, then snap back into focus. One evening, he stood in front of the mirror in the bathroom, his reflection strangely out of sync with his movements. He blinked, shook his head, and the moment passed. But something was changing. He could feel it.

Theo, as always, kept his emotions in check. He was calm, cool, and collected, but beneath the surface, something was shifting. He found himself questioning everything—the group's decisions, the notebook's power, and even his place among them.

The strange events continued. At night, he would hear noises, small things like the creak of floorboards or the sound of something dragging across the floor, but when he investigated, he found nothing.

And yet... the dread lingered. He could feel it, just out of reach, like a whisper in the dark.

It was late one evening when the tension finally reached its breaking point. The group sat around Zara's table, the notebook locked securely in its box, but the weight of it hung in the air like a storm ready to break.

"I can't do this anymore," Max blurted out, his voice shaking. "I thought it would be easier, but it's not. It's... it's getting worse."

"We're all feeling it," Ellie said, her voice low.

"We need to talk about this," Zara said, her voice cracking. "We can't keep pretending everything's fine. The notebook... it's messing with us."

Jake nodded, his usual humour absent. "Yeah. It's like it's getting inside our heads."

Theo crossed his arms. "So, what now? Do we confront it? Do we—"

"No," Ellie interrupted, her voice firm. "We don't. Not yet."

"We're already too far gone," Max whispered.

The room fell into silence.

As they sat there, the weight of their words settling in, the silence grew oppressive. No one knew what to do. No one had an answer. The notebook had been sealed away, but its influence was still very much alive, twisting their thoughts, their emotions, and their relationships.

"Maybe... maybe we should destroy it," Max said, breaking the silence.

"No," Ellie said, her voice sharp. "We agreed. It's too dangerous."

"But what's the point of keeping it locked away if it's still tearing us apart?" Max asked.

"I agree," Zara said quietly. "It's not just about the notebook anymore. It's about us. We're... we're falling apart."

Ellie looked at them all and for the first time, she wondered if they were already too far gone.

Ellie left Zara's house that night, the box tucked under her arm, her mind a whirlwind of uncertainty. The decision to take the notebook home had been a suggestion, one that felt right in the moment, though doubt had already begun to gnaw at her. She hadn't told the others yet, but deep down, Ellie knew she felt a strange pull to be near the notebook—to keep it close, to understand it, to control it in ways they hadn't yet tried.

As she entered her house, the familiar warmth of home settled over her, but it was a comfort that felt fragile, almost fleeting. The box, secured with the lock they had wished for, sat on the dining table, a silent presence that weighed heavily on her.

Hours passed in a blur, the evening stretching into night. Ellie tried to settle into a routine, checking in with her family, watching TV, and attempting to focus on her art. But no matter how hard she tried to distract herself, her thoughts kept returning to the box.

It was as if it were calling her.

170

She excused herself from the living room, her heart beating faster as she made her way to the dining table. The box sat there, pristine and untouched, the lock gleaming in the dim light. The wish they had made echoed in her mind—*that only they could open it together.*

And yet, Ellie felt a strange tug in her chest, a desire. She approached the table, her fingers brushing the cool wood, and without thinking, she reached for the box.

Her hand shook as she touched the lock, and for a moment, she hesitated. The words of the wish ran through her mind again—*only together, as a group*—but it didn't stop her. She tried to unlock the case, expecting it to resist, to hold fast. It should have been impossible to open. But when she applied the slightest pressure, the lock clicked open as if it had never been secured.

Ellie's breath caught in her throat.

The lock had worked perfectly when they'd left Zara's house, when they had sealed it as a group. She had seen it with her own eyes. So why was it now opening so easily? Was it a mistake? Had the lock somehow malfunctioned?

No. Something was wrong.

Her fingers trembled as she lifted the lid, the soft creak of the wood filling the quiet room. Inside, the notebook lay untouched, just as it had been. But something about the air around it felt different, charged, as though the box itself were alive.

Ellie stared down at the notebook, the weight of her decision crashing down on her. The group's wish had been clear. They had agreed that only they, as a collective, would open the box, that they would keep it locked until they had a plan. But now, here she was, alone, opening it without any of them.

A pang of guilt gripped her heart, but alongside it was a strange sense of triumph. It was as though the notebook was beckoning her, as though it were... inviting her to see what lay beyond the surface.

Ellie's fingers hovered over the pages, and she was struck by the way the notebook seemed to shimmer in the low light. Without thinking, she opened it, her mind full of questions she hadn't even dared to voice aloud before.

As she flipped the first few pages, nothing happened. It was the same, the paper soft under her fingers. But as Ellie reached the middle, she noticed a subtle change. The pages began to shift, rearranging themselves in ways she couldn't explain. The notebook seemed to be alive, pulsing with a rhythm of its own, as though responding to her touch.

Ellie could feel it—an invisible force pushing and pulling at her, urging her to continue. It was as if the notebook knew her, knew her thoughts, her desires, her fears. It was feeding off her emotions, responding to the quiet storm inside her.

A low hum began to fill the air around her. She closed her eyes, feeling an overwhelming sense of connection to the notebook—like it was part of her now. The pull was undeniable. She could feel the power coursing through her veins, the rush of possibilities flooding her thoughts.

She could make a wish. She could make everything right again.

But the warning, the memories of the consequences, lingered in her mind. She had seen firsthand how each wish twisted into something unrecognizable, how the cost could be devastating.

But what if...?

Ellie's heart raced as she stared down at the notebook. There was something so... alluring about it, something that promised to make things better, to take away all the uncertainty and fear. The group had been struggling to figure out what to do next, but Ellie felt like she had the answer in her hands.

All she had to do was write.

One small wish.

What could it hurt?

The temptation was too strong. Ellie's fingers hovered over the page, her mind spinning with all the possibilities. She could wish for peace, for safety, for happiness—things she hadn't felt in a long time. And she knew, deep down, that she could do it alone. She didn't need anyone else to make it happen.

But then the guilt came back, sharper this time. What about the others? What about the promise we made?

She clenched her fists, her mind torn between the desire for relief and the responsibility she felt toward her friends. Could she really do this alone?

And as if sensing her hesitation, the notebook seemed to shift again, the pages fluttering as if to urge her on. The air grew heavier, the hum vibrating in her chest.

Ellie closed the notebook with a sudden snap, the weight of the decision nearly suffocating her. She stared at the box, her hands trembling as she set the notebook back inside. She couldn't do it—not yet. But the pull was still there, lingering, whispering.

You can have anything you want.

But deep down, Ellie knew the price was never worth it. The power to make wishes might be in her hands, but the consequences—those were real, and they were still out of her control.

With a deep breath, Ellie locked the box again, her mind heavy with uncertainty. She needed to talk to the group. They needed to decide together—because the notebook was no longer just a thing. It was a living force, one that would not rest until it had its way.

And Ellie knew, with growing dread, that they hadn't seen the last of its power.

The days following Ellie's solo encounter with the notebook were clouded with a mixture of guilt and unease. She had locked it away again, but the weight of her actions lingered, heavy and unshakable. She had broken the rule—what they had all agreed to do together. She had opened the box, and more importantly, she had opened the notebook. Alone.

It was hard to know what to say to the group. How could she explain what had happened? How could she justify her decision when, deep down, she knew it had been a choice made out of temptation, out of the promise of control over something that felt too big to ignore?

Ellie had always prided herself on her ability to listen, to understand the needs of those around her. But this time, the silence that filled her was suffocating. The guilt gnawed at her, and she couldn't help but wonder if it was a sign of something deeper, something that might have already begun to erode the trust that held the group together.

The decision was made for her when Zara called, her voice steady but with an undercurrent of concern.
"We need to talk," she said, not waiting for Ellie to respond. "Come to my house. Everyone will be there."
Ellie's stomach tightened. She could already imagine the questions, the looks of confusion and disappointment. She had known this was coming. They had all felt the strain, the tension growing between them, but now it was real. Now, it had become something that couldn't be avoided.

Zara's house was quiet when Ellie arrived, the other members of the group already gathered around the table. Max's nervous energy was palpable, his fingers tapping restlessly on the

178

edge of the table, while Theo leaned back in his chair, his eyes narrowed in quiet suspicion. Jake's usual light-heartedness was gone; instead, there was an almost tangible air of tension about him.

Zara didn't waste any time.

"Ellie," she began, her tone even but firm, "we need to talk about the notebook."

Ellie's heart skipped a beat. She had prepared for this, but nothing could have prepared her for how it felt to face them all, their eyes filled with unspoken questions.

"I opened it," Ellie said, her voice barely above a whisper. She felt the weight of her admission crash over her like a tidal wave. "I opened the box. I thought—"

"You thought?" Zara interrupted, her voice sharp. "You thought it was okay to open it alone? After everything we agreed on?"

Ellie's chest tightened, the words feeling like they were caught in her throat. She had no excuse. No good reason for breaking the trust they had all worked so hard to establish.

"I... I couldn't stop myself. I felt... I felt like I needed to know what was inside. Like if I didn't do it, I might lose the chance forever. I thought I could control it."

Jake let out a harsh laugh, but it lacked its usual humour. "Control it? Are you kidding? You know what this thing does, right? You think it's just going to let you control it?"

Ellie winced. She had heard the tone in his voice before—the one that hinted at something darker. She had made a mistake, and now it was more than just a mistake. It was a breach of trust.

"I'm sorry," Ellie said, her voice breaking. "I should've waited. I should've told you. I didn't mean to—"

"You don't get it, do you?" Max cut in, his voice unusually sharp. "This isn't about what you meant to do. It's about what you did. You went behind our backs, and now none of us can trust that we're on the same page."

The words stung, harder than she'd expected. The truth of them settled over her, cold and painful.

Ellie looked at the group, her eyes flicking from one face to the next. It was clear that they were all hurt—not just by her actions, but by the sudden shift in the dynamic between them. What had once been a tight-knit bond, built on mutual understanding and shared experiences, now felt fractured.

Theo leaned forward, his arms crossed tightly over his chest. "So, what's next, then? You open the notebook alone. What, you think you can just do whatever you want with it?"

Ellie's gaze dropped to the table, her fingers fiddling with the edge of her sleeve. "No. I didn't think that. I—"

"You can't just decide to play with it by yourself," Theo continued, his voice low and sharp. "You didn't just break a rule, Ellie. You broke our trust. And that's not something you can just fix with an apology."

Ellie swallowed hard. She knew it was true. She had never felt more alone, despite the group being right in front of her. It was as though the space between them had expanded, stretching wide enough that even their shared history couldn't bridge it.

Zara's expression softened, but only slightly. "The notebook is dangerous, Ellie. It's not something you can control. We made a promise that we would approach this together. We *needed* to do this together. But now... now I don't know what to believe."

Max was quiet for a long moment, his eyes darting from Ellie to the others. Finally, he spoke, his voice barely above a whisper. "What if it's already too late? What if the notebook has already done something to us? We don't even know what could happen next."

His words hit Ellie like a blow. He was right. They didn't know. None of them did. They had only scratched the surface of the notebook's power and it seemed to change, to grow more unpredictable.

"I'm sorry," Ellie said again, her voice thick with regret. "I didn't think it through. I didn't mean to—"

Zara held up a hand to stop her. "We all made mistakes, Ellie. I'm not here to lecture you, but we need to be honest with each other. The trust we had before... it's not the same now. And I don't know if we can just pick up where we left off."

The room fell into silence, the weight of Zara's words settling over them. Trust, once broken, was difficult to rebuild. Ellie could feel the distance between her and the group expanding further, a chasm that felt impossible to cross.

It was Jake who broke the silence, his voice quieter than usual. "Look, we're not going to fix this in one conversation. But if we're going to get through this—if we're going to even think about using the notebook again—we need to start rebuilding trust. All of us."

Ellie looked up at Jake, surprised by the calmness in his voice. Despite the tension, despite the hurt, he was trying to offer a path forward. Maybe there was hope, after all.

Zara nodded slowly, her expression softening. "We need to be a team again. And that means being open. We can't have secrets. We need to talk. To trust each other."

Ellie's heart felt a little lighter, though the weight of her mistake still lingered. She wasn't sure how they would get there, how they could repair what had been broken. But in that moment, Ellie realised that the foundation of their friendship, their shared journey, would only survive if they could rebuild the trust they had once had.

And that would take time.

The tension in the room had not entirely faded, but the storm of anger and frustration began to settle, leaving behind a quiet but uncomfortable stillness. Ellie, still feeling the weight of her actions, kept her eyes fixed on the table, unable to meet anyone's gaze. She could feel the lingering mistrust, the distance between her and the group. It wasn't just the notebook that had caused the fracture—it was the betrayal of their unspoken bond, the one that had held them together since this all began.

But then, as they all sat in silence, a strange thing began to happen. The sharp edges of their earlier arguments began to soften, replaced by a quiet realisation that perhaps there was more to this situation than just Ellie's mistake.

Zara was the first to break the silence, her voice quiet, almost contemplative. "Wait a second."

Ellie looked up, startled, but Zara wasn't looking at her—she was staring at the box, her eyes narrowed in thought. "The lock," Zara said slowly. "It shouldn't have opened. The wish was clear, wasn't it? *Only together* could we open it."

Max, who had been quietly fiddling with his glasses, spoke up.
"Right. We made the wish. It wasn't supposed to be possible
for anyone to open it alone. It was supposed to be foolproof."
Theo leaned forward, a frown tugging at his lips. "So, what
does that mean? If the lock should have kept it closed... how
was Ellie able to open it?"
Ellie's heart skipped a beat as the implications began to sink
in. She had assumed it was her own actions, her own
weakness that had caused the lock to give way. But now, with
the others pointing out the obvious flaw in the plan, she
realised that something else was at play.

The room fell quiet again, but this time the silence was
charged with an uncomfortable energy. The lock had been a
safeguard, something they had all trusted to protect the
notebook. The fact that it had failed—opened, despite the
clear instructions of their wish—suggested something far
more troubling than Ellie's lapse in judgment.

Jake, who had been unusually silent up until that point, finally spoke, his voice low and serious. "So, the notebook... is it messing with the lock? Or did we do something wrong? Because if the notebook's got the power to bypass our wish... then we're in deep."

Zara's eyes flicked to Ellie, and for the first time, Ellie saw something that wasn't just frustration or disappointment. There was fear. Not just fear of what they had already unleashed, but fear of what else might be waiting for them, what else they hadn't even considered yet.

"I don't think we *did* anything wrong," Zara said slowly, as though testing the idea in her mind. "The lock worked before. We all saw it. But now... it's like the notebook just... overrode it."

Theo, always the sceptic, seemed lost in thought. He hadn't said much, but the flicker of concern in his eyes told a different story. "I don't know, but the fact that the lock didn't hold—that's not just a glitch. There's something more happening here. The notebook is changing. *It* is controlling things now, not us."

Ellie felt the weight of the truth settle heavily on her chest. The notebook was evolving. It wasn't just an object anymore—it was alive, changing, adapting, pushing the limits of their control. And now, with the lock broken, it felt like they had lost their grip on it entirely.

Zara exhaled slowly, her fingers resting lightly on the table. "We didn't account for this. We didn't think about the possibility that the notebook could influence the lock, could override our wishes in ways we didn't expect."

Ellie, still reeling from the realisation, nodded. "I—I didn't even think about that. I thought... I thought the lock would hold, that we could be in control, that we could protect it."

"None of us expected this," Jake said, his voice unusually serious. "But that doesn't change the fact that it happened."

There was a pause, and for a moment, the group seemed to sink into a collective contemplation. The notebook had proven time and again that it wasn't just a simple object; it was a force that bent reality to its will. And now, with the lock bypassed, it was clear that the consequences were far more serious than any of them had realised.

Max was the first to break the silence. "So, what do we do now? If the lock's not reliable, then how do we keep it contained? How do we make sure it doesn't cause more damage?"

Zara rubbed her temples, the frustration evident in her expression.

"But we can't just *destroy* it," Ellie said, her voice quiet but firm. "It's too dangerous. We can't risk what might happen if we do that. We need to find another way."

Theo looked at her sharply. "And you think just keeping it around, locked up, is going to be safe? It's already proven that it can bypass our safeguards. If we're not careful—"

"I know," Ellie interrupted, her voice steady despite the turmoil inside her. "I'm not suggesting we just keep it around for nothing. But we can't jump to conclusions. We need to think carefully about our next steps."

The room was still, the weight of their collective responsibility settling on them like a heavy fog. They had opened Pandora's box, and now they were faced with the consequences of their choices.

Zara's voice broke the silence again, quieter now, but resolute. "We'll keep it locked. We'll study it. But we'll never open it alone again. Not like that."

Ellie nodded in agreement, the guilt still hanging over her like a dark cloud. But Zara's words felt like a small anchor, a sliver of hope during the chaos they had created.

For the first time in days, Ellie felt like they were all on the same page again, like there was a way forward—difficult, uncertain, but together.

It was clear now that the notebook had the power to change everything, to bend reality and alter the very fabric of their world. But it was also clear that they couldn't let it control them.

The lock had failed. The notebook had already begun to show its true nature. But they still had a choice—one they would have to make together.

And Ellie knew, as they all stood there, facing the notebook once again, that their journey wasn't over. It was just beginning.

Chapter 12 – Return of the wish

The room felt different the morning after their intense discussion. The air was thick with the unspoken tension that had followed Ellie's breach of trust, but there was also a new, quieter determination among them. The notebook had revealed a side of itself they hadn't expected, and it had left them all shaken. But with the morning light streaming through the windows of Zara's living room, there was a sense of clarity.

Later that day, the group gathered around the table, their eyes drifting warily toward the wooden box where the notebook was locked away. A strange, almost palpable energy seemed to stir in the air—a hum that buzzed at the edges of their awareness. The room felt charged, as if the notebook was still watching them, still waiting for the right moment to reveal more.

Zara was the first to speak, her voice steady but with a note of resolve. "We need to understand what's happening with the notebook. We can't just keep reacting to it. We need to figure out how it works, how it's manipulating us, so we can stop it."

Max's eyes flicked nervously to the box. "But what if—what if it's already too late? What if the notebook's already done something?"

"We don't know that" Zara replied firmly, her gaze unwavering. "We can't act out of fear. We need to take control."

Just as the words left Zara's mouth, a faint sound echoed from the wooden box. It was so quiet, so subtle, that at first, none of them were sure they had heard it at all. But then it came again, a soft scraping sound, like the rustling of paper. It was a noise too deliberate to be a coincidence. The notebook was moving.

The group froze, eyes widening in horror. Theo was the first to stand, his body tense with sudden alarm. "What the hell was that?"

Zara's fingers twitched, instinctively reaching for the box, but she stopped herself before touching it. "We need to be sure. Don't open it yet."

Max swallowed hard, his throat tight with unease. "Maybe it's reacting to what we said.

The noise from the box came again, louder now, unmistakable. The group exchanged uncertain glances, each of them struggling with the urge to act, to open the box and see what was going on inside.

But as the tension reached its peak, the box shifted on its own. A faint glow began to seep from the cracks between the wood, faint at first, but growing brighter with each passing moment.

Ellie's heart raced. She could feel the notebook pulling her in, calling to her with an almost hypnotic force. Her heart pounded in her chest. She had thought that once the notebook was locked away, everything would be fine. The

194

room was thick with a charged silence, the air practically vibrating with tension as the group stared in disbelief. Without warning, the lock that had once secured the notebook snapped. The wooden box jerked open, almost violently, as though it had been waiting for this moment. The notebook lay inside, resting on the velvet-lined base, its pages seemingly untouched.

But something was different.

Ellie's breath caught in her throat as the notebook seemed to pulse, as though it was alive, responding to the energy in the room. There was no denying it now—the notebook was no longer just an object they had to protect. It was a force, one that was beyond their understanding.

The group instinctively took a collective step back, but the notebook didn't stop. A faint, eerie glow began to emanate from the pages. It wasn't bright, but it was there, a sickly, almost unnatural hue. The pages turned of their own accord, flipping rapidly until they stopped at one particular page. The glow intensified, now spilling over the edges of the notebook and into the surrounding air.

A cold chill swept through the room, and the group shivered, though none of them dared to speak. The message on the page was clear etched in ink that seemed to shimmer as it formed.

"I have watched you.

You think you control me, but it is I who control you.

You made your wishes. Now, you will learn the cost.

To each wish, a price must be paid. The price is not always visible, but it is always real.

Do you think you can escape? Do you think you can lock me away and forget? I will not let you.

Your desires, your hopes, your dreams—they will come to me, and I will return them to you, twisted and broken. But not today.

You will face a choice. A choice between *more* and *nothing*.

Choose wisely.

For I am *always* watching."

The words hung in the air like a death sentence. The chill in the room intensified, and Ellie's heart pounded in her chest as she tried to make sense of what she had just read. The notebook wasn't just granting wishes—it was manipulating them. It wasn't offering them a gift; it was *feeding* on their desires, their weaknesses. The idea that their wishes were now "twisted and broken" gnawed at her, a terrible warning.

Max was the first to speak, his voice shaky with fear. "What... what does that mean? Twisted? Broken?"

Jake's usual playfulness was gone, replaced by a deep seriousness that sent a ripple of unease through the group. "It's saying the cost of every wish is going to come back at us. And... we don't know what it'll be."

Zara clenched her fists, her jaw tightening as she processed the message. "The notebook isn't just offering us a deal—it's forcing us into one. We made wishes, and now it's going to make us *pay*."

Theo, always sceptical, was uncharacteristically quiet, his eyes narrowed as he studied the notebook. He wasn't sure what to believe, but even he couldn't ignore the ominous aura that now seemed to suffuse the room.

Ellie took a step forward, her heart racing, her thoughts a whirlwind. She felt the weight of the message pressing down on her—*you will learn the cost*. Jake's wish, the one he had made for happiness, suddenly felt far more sinister. She had seen its effect on others—the way Max had paid the price for Jake's joy. But now, the notebook was implying that the cost wasn't over. That it would keep coming back, again and again.

"What do we do now?" she asked softly, more to herself than to anyone else.

Zara looked at the notebook, her face a mask of determination. "We keep it locked. We don't make any more wishes. We must figure out what's happening, what this thing really wants."

But Ellie couldn't shake the feeling that they were already too far gone. The notebook was in their lives now, and they had no idea how deeply it had already entwined itself in their fate.

The group was silent, lost in their own thoughts, the words of the message echoing in their minds.

Ellie had thought that keeping the notebook locked away would be enough. That the hardest part was over. But now, with the glowing message in front of them, the reality of their situation had shifted. The notebook wasn't just a mysterious object. It was a living entity, and it had power over them that they couldn't yet comprehend.

Jake, ever the wildcard, spoke up after a long pause. "So, it's giving us a choice. More or nothing. What do you think it means?"

Zara frowned, her brow furrowed in thought. "I think it's playing on our desires. It's offering us *something*, but it's going to cost us more than we can predict. If we make any more wishes, it will keep coming back for payment."

Max's voice was tight, his anxiety palpable. "And what if we choose 'nothing'? What does that mean? What does the notebook take then?"

Ellie had a sinking feeling in her stomach. The notebook had already shown them how it could warp their reality. If they refused its power, would they find themselves in a worse situation?

Zara stood up slowly, taking a deep breath. "Whatever happens, we can't use it. We don't know the full extent of what this thing can do. We need to find a way to break free from its control."

"But what if we can't?" Max's voice trembled. "What if it's too late?"

There was no answer to that question—not yet. But the group knew they had to make a choice soon. The notebook was still in the room with them, its pages pulsing faintly, waiting for them to act.

As the group stood around the open box, they realised one thing: the notebook had already taken root in their lives. Whether they wanted to face it or not, they had no choice but to deal with it.

Ellie's mind raced as she looked at the glowing pages. The notebook had given them a choice: more or nothing. But no matter what they chose, the cost was clear—it would always come back.

And for the first time, Ellie understood the full depth of the notebook's power: it wasn't just a tool for getting what they wanted. It was a reminder that every wish, every desire, came

with a price—a price that could never be truly escaped.

Chapter 13 – a Glimpse of the past

The group had spent days locked in silence, their minds spinning with the weight of the notebook's cryptic message. They had agreed, at least temporarily, to leave the notebook alone, but that didn't mean they could stop thinking about it. It lingered in the back of their minds, a shadow that followed them wherever they went.

But as the days passed, a strange unease began to settle in— something wasn't quite right. Ellie felt it more acutely than the others. The weight of the notebook's influence seemed to grow heavier with each passing moment. It felt as though it had left a mark on them, one they couldn't see but could sense in the way they looked at each other, the way their emotions seemed to be tied to an invisible thread that stretched between them. And it wasn't just the group that was feeling it. Their pets—Luna, Zara's dog, and the others—were acting strangely too, more skittish, more on edge.

The group had trusted Ellie again with keeping the notebook safely stored away.

That night, Ellie found herself unable to sleep. She lay awake in bed, staring at the ceiling, wondering if it was really the notebook that was making her feel so unsettled or if it was something else entirely. She had barely realised it, but her hand had moved to the drawer beside her bed, the one where she kept the notebook's wooden box hidden away. Without even thinking, she reached for it.

When her fingers touched the smooth wood of the box, a sharp twinge of something—guilt, curiosity, fear—shot through her.

Something shifted within her, a spark of something that made her feel as though she were being drawn into the depths of a mystery too vast to comprehend.

The temptation was too much. Without fully understanding

why, Ellie found herself gently prying open the box, her heart

thumping in her chest. She had promised the group that she

wouldn't touch it again—not without them. But the pull of the

notebook was undeniable. It had done something to her. It

was as if the book had a power over her, over all of them, that

no one had fully grasped yet.

The notebook was nestled against the soft velvet lining of the

box. Its cover was smooth and unassuming, but Ellie felt a

sense of foreboding wash over her as she carefully slid it out.

She had to know more—she had to understand what was

really happening.

As her fingers grazed the pages, the familiar weight of the

notebook felt different this time. It didn't feel like a simple

book. It felt like a vessel—one that held something ancient,

something beyond her understanding. She didn't open it, but

she could feel it *inside* her mind, as though it were beckoning her, urging her to look closer.

And then, without warning, the pages of the notebook began to turn. Slowly at first, like the whispers of a long-forgotten voice. The faint, eerie glow returned, spilling from the edges of the book and casting strange shadows in the room. Ellie's breath caught in her throat.

But this time, the words on the page were different.

The words formed before her, twisting and shifting like a living thing.

"I have watched your desires. I have seen your fears. I have seen the choices you make."

The words continued to appear, as though the notebook itself were speaking, recounting something from long ago.

"There were others before you, others who made their own choices. Some were wise, others... not so much."

Ellie's heart raced. She could feel the air around her grow

colder as the words continued to spill from the pages.

"You think you are the first to seek power from me? To make

a wish and expect nothing in return? You are mistaken."

The text stopped abruptly, and Ellie's fingers hovered over the

pages, but the notebook continued its dark narrative.

Suddenly, the room around Ellie seemed to warp and fade, as

though the very walls of her bedroom were dissolving. The air

grew thick with a sense of something *old*, ancient even, and

Ellie felt as though she were being transported somewhere far

away, somewhere she couldn't quite place. The world around

her shifted again, and she found herself in an unfamiliar

setting—an old, dimly lit room.

She could hear the soft scratch of a quill on parchment, the

low murmur of voices, and the unmistakable sound of

someone else's heartbeat, steady but anxious. A shadow

moved past her, and she gasped as she realised that she was no longer alone.

A figure stepped into view. A woman, her face obscured by the heavy hood of a cloak, but her hands were visible, trembling as she held a small book—*the notebook*. Ellie's breath caught in her throat. This was impossible.

The figure spoke, though her voice was distant, as though coming from a long time ago. "The cost of every wish... it always returns. Always."

Ellie could feel her heart racing as the woman closed the book, her hands tightening around it. There was something *frantic* in her movements, as though she had made a terrible mistake, one that she was trying to undo.

But it was too late. The woman vanished as quickly as she had appeared, leaving Ellie alone in the room.

The vision around her flickered, and Ellie was thrust back into her own room, gasping for breath, her fingers still trembling against the pages of the notebook.

The notebook had shown her a glimpse of the past—a

warning from someone who had come before her. Someone

who had made the same mistakes they were making now.

The cost of their wishes was always *returned*, and no matter

how they tried to lock it away, the notebook would keep

drawing them back in.

Ellie stared down at the pages, her mind reeling from the

vision she had just witnessed. She couldn't deny it anymore.

The notebook wasn't just an object of power—it was

something far more dangerous. And whatever had happened

to those who came before them, whatever mistakes they had

made, Ellie knew they had to avoid them.

But could they?

Ellie closed the notebook gently, placing it back in the box and

securing the lock. Her heart still raced, the vision lingering in

her mind. She didn't know what the past had been like for

those who had used the notebook before her, but she knew

one thing for sure: they had been just like her. They had made

a wish, sought something they wanted, and paid the price.

But this time, Ellie was determined that she wouldn't make the

same mistake.

Chapter 14 – The shadow's grasp

The vision had unsettled Ellie, but it was nothing compared to the unease she felt in the days that followed. The notebook was locked away again, but its presence was still palpable, a constant shadow hanging over the group. Ellie couldn't shake the feeling that it was *waiting*—waiting for them to make another move, to make another wish, to give in to temptation. But it wasn't just the notebook that felt wrong. Something in the air had shifted. It was subtle at first—little things. Luna, Ellie's grey tabby cat, was more withdrawn than usual, curling up in the farthest corners of the house, staring at the walls as if something was watching her. Zara's dog, a loyal golden retriever named Scout, had taken to barking at nothing, growling into the empty space where no one was.

And then there were the dreams.

Every night, Ellie was plagued by vivid nightmares. Nightmares that blurred the line between reality and the strange visions she had seen in the notebook. In these dreams, she saw herself—only it wasn't her. It was someone else, someone who had been here before, someone who had made the same choices. She was trapped in a dark, empty room, with shadows closing in from every direction. The figure—Ellie, or someone like her—scrambled for the notebook, desperate to escape the darkness that encircled her.

The shadows seemed to stretch out of the walls, whispering her name.

"Ellie... Come... make your wish."

She awoke with a start, gasping for breath, the weight of the dream lingering like a fog in her mind.

The group met at Zara's house the following evening, but the usual camaraderie felt strained. The weight of their shared burden hung between them, making even the most casual conversation feel forced. Ellie hadn't told the others about the dream—about the shadow, the whisper—but she could see in their eyes that they felt it too.

Max, ever the realist, was the first to speak. His voice was quieter than usual, filled with uncertainty. "Has anyone else... felt like something is watching us?"

Theo, who had been unusually quiet, nodded. His face was unreadable, but there was an unmistakable tension in his posture, as if he were waiting for something to happen. "I don't know if it's just me, but it feels like... like the air is thick. Like there's something pressing in on us."

Zara looked around the room, her expression hardening as she scanned the faces of her friends. She had been the one to argue most vehemently against using the notebook again, but even she couldn't deny the creeping feeling of dread that had been growing over the past few days. The strange behaviour of their pets, the unsettling dreams, the unease in their very bones—it was all connected, and it was all pointing to one thing: the notebook.

"Maybe... maybe we've been too careful," Ellie said quietly, her voice betraying a hint of fear. "Maybe we've ignored something important. We've locked the notebook away, but what if that's not enough? What if it's already too late?"

Zara's eyes narrowed as she considered the possibility. "If we've been ignoring it, maybe that's what it wants. It's playing on our fears, making us question everything we do. But we need to figure out how to stop it before it takes over completely."

A long silence followed her words, one that felt heavy and thick, like something was waiting to pounce. They all felt it— this creeping presence, this shadow that seemed to loom just out of sight.

"I think we need to take it back to where it all started," Max said suddenly, breaking the silence. His eyes were wide, and though his voice wavered, there was a newfound determination in it. "We can't just keep running from it. We need to find out where the notebook came from, who used it before us, what happened to them."

Ellie's heart skipped a beat at his words. The idea of delving into the past—of understanding who had made the same choices they had—felt like the only way forward. They couldn't keep ignoring the notebook's origins, its power. They needed to face it head-on.

But that wasn't enough. They needed to understand the full extent of what they were up against, and they needed to stop whatever dark force seemed to be clawing its way into their lives.

"I agree," Zara said, her voice firm, though the uncertainty in her eyes couldn't be hidden. "But we can't just go in blindly. We need to be prepared. We need to figure out how to break this thing's grip on us before it completely takes over."

Ellie nodded slowly, but the weight of what they were about to do settled heavily on her chest. She could feel the pressure in the room mounting, like a storm that was about to break. They were no longer just five teenagers trying to make sense of something bizarre. They were facing something far darker, something they weren't sure they could control.

The air felt even thicker as the group began to plan their next move, but Ellie couldn't shake the feeling that whatever they did, they were already too far into the shadow's grasp. And it was pulling them deeper.

Later that night, as Ellie walked home alone, her senses were heightened. She could feel it again—the weight of something in the air, the sensation of being watched. But it wasn't just in her mind. She turned quickly as she heard a faint rustling sound behind her, but there was nothing there. Only the quiet of the empty street.

Luna, Ellie's cat, was waiting for her at the door, but something in the cat's posture made Ellie pause. Luna's fur stood on end, her green eyes wide, unblinking. She was staring at something—or *someone*—just out of view.

Ellie's heart pounded in her chest as she slowly opened the door, but the strange feeling lingered, pressing on her chest like a weight she couldn't shake.

She didn't know what it was, but the shadows were getting closer. And no matter how hard she tried to escape, they were always there, just out of sight, pulling at the edges of her reality. The next evening the group met again at Zara's house. The room was thick with tension as the group sat around Zara's living room.

Ellie hadn't said much since their last meeting. The vision she'd seen, the haunting glimpse of the past, had rattled her to the core. The shadow, the whispers—everything about the notebook felt like a warning. But it wasn't just the notebook that was unsettling her now. It was the fact that the journal Ellie's grandmother had kept for years had somehow been connected to it.

The first thing Ellie did when she arrived at Zara's house was pull out the old journal. It was bound in faded leather, the pages yellowed with age, and the smell of old paper hung in the air as she carefully opened it. The handwriting was elegant, almost archaic, and as she began to read, she could feel the weight of the words bearing down on her.

"I've kept this journal for years, and though I've hesitated to write my thoughts down, I now see that I must. For the sake of the family and the ones I hold dear, I must record the truth. The truth of the notebook that I found, and the wishes I made."

Ellie's breath caught in her throat as she read those words. The truth? Her grandmother had known about the notebook? Ellie had thought it was simply a coincidence that the box had been hidden away in the loft, untouched for so long. But now it was clear that her grandmother had been involved with the notebook too.

Her hands shook as she turned the page.

As the group gathered around, Ellie shared the journal's contents with them, her voice barely above a whisper as she read aloud. The more they read, the more they realised that her grandmother had been just as drawn to the notebook as they had been. She had stumbled upon it when she was younger, much like Ellie had, and had made her own wish. The journal detailed her grandmother's experience with the notebook's power. She had wished for a life of ease, a life where she never had to worry about anything again. At first, everything had seemed perfect. But then, just as the group had discovered, things began to unravel. Her wish, like all wishes made with the notebook, came with a price.

Her grandmother wrote, "The things I asked for came with more than I could ever have anticipated. The happiness, the ease—it was never as it seemed. Others around me suffered, and I couldn't undo it. The notebook's power is both a blessing and a curse, and now I see that I am not the first to fall prey to its temptation."

Ellie paused for a moment, her voice catching in her throat. Her grandmother had experienced the same consequences they were facing now—the same darkness, the same cost. The more they read, the more they realised that their actions were not isolated. This had happened before. People had used the notebook, made their wishes, and then lived to regret it.

As Ellie turned the page, she found an entry that seemed to echo the vision she had seen. The journal entry was dated many years ago, long before Ellie had been born, but the words seemed eerily familiar.

"I must hide the notebook. I must ensure that it does not fall into the wrong hands. It has a way of drawing people in, of making them think they can control it, but they cannot. I do not know how much longer I can keep it locked away, but I must try. I hope that my children, and my children's children, will never have to face the temptation of the notebook. The price of wishes is too high, and I have seen what it does to people. The darkness it leaves behind is beyond anything I could have ever imagined."

Ellie felt a chill run down her spine. Her grandmother had known—she had known the danger and had tried to protect the family. But somehow, the notebook had found its way back into their lives.

"We have to stop it," Zara said, breaking the silence. Her voice was firm, but there was an underlying fear in it. "We can't let the same thing happen to us, to anyone else. We need to know how to break the cycle, how to stop it from spreading."

Ellie nodded. Her heart ached as she thought of her grandmother. She had tried to protect her family, to shield them from the notebook's curse. And yet, here they were, caught in the same trap.

The group spent the next few hours poring over the journal, searching for anything that might help them. There were mentions of attempts to destroy the notebook, to lock it away, but each time it had found its way back into someone's hands. No matter how hard they tried, the notebook's influence was unstoppable.

But then, buried deep within the pages, Ellie found something that gave her hope. A final entry, written just days before her grandmother's death, offered a glimmer of a solution.

"The notebook can be locked away, hidden, or destroyed, but its influence will always remain. The only way to truly sever the connection is to break the cycle. It requires a sacrifice—a choice that cannot be undone. The one who made the wish must be willing to let go of what they have gained, to give up the happiness, the ease, the power they've sought. Only then will the curse be broken. But be warned, the cost of this final act is unknown. The notebook will not relinquish its hold easily."

Ellie's eyes widened as she read those words aloud. A sacrifice. The notebook had to be *given up*, but the price was unknown.

Ellie closed the journal, her mind whirling with the revelation. The answer they had been searching for was right there in her grandmother's words. The notebook could only be stopped if they were willing to let go of the very things it had promised them.

But the question remained: Could they?

The group sat in stunned silence, the weight of what they had learned settling heavily on their shoulders. The stakes had never been higher, and the cost of their choices loomed larger than ever.

But one thing was clear. The only way forward was to break the cycle. And to do that, they had to be ready to make the sacrifice.

Chapter 15 – a Moment of clarity

The evening sunlight filtered through Zara's living room window, casting a golden glow over the group as they sat in contemplative silence. Ellie, holding her grandmother's journal, stared at its aged leather cover, her thoughts spinning. The weight of their discovery hung in the air like a storm cloud.

"We can't just pretend this didn't happen," Zara said finally, her voice steady but quiet. "We have the answer now. We know how to stop the notebook. The question is whether we're willing to pay the price."

Theo leaned back in his chair, arms crossed, his usual scepticism sharp in his voice. "And what exactly is the price? We're taking advice from a journal written decades ago. For all we know, the 'sacrifice' could mean anything."

"Does it matter?" Max piped up, nervously adjusting his glasses. "If it stops more people from being hurt, isn't it worth it?"

"That's easy to say," Theo shot back, his tone colder now. "But what if the cost is worse than we think? What if it takes more than we can give?"

Ellie took a deep breath, steadying herself. She wasn't used to speaking up in moments like these, but something about the journal—about her grandmother's words—made her feel an unshakable connection to the group's shared burden.

"I don't think my grandmother would've written those words lightly," she said softly, but with conviction. "She lived with the notebook for years, knowing its power, its consequences. She knew what it did to people—what it could do to us. And she still believed there was a way to stop it."

The group turned their attention to Ellie. Even Theo, who rarely masked his doubts, seemed intrigued by the quiet certainty in her voice.

Ellie continued, "If we don't do something, we're leaving it for someone else to deal with. Someone who might not stop at wishes for happiness or curiosity. Someone who might destroy lives without a second thought. That's not a risk we can take."

Jake, who had been unusually quiet, suddenly grinned—a grin that didn't reach his eyes. "So, we're supposed to be the big heroes, huh? Save the world from an evil notebook?" His tone was joking, but the tension in his posture betrayed his unease.

"Not heroes," Zara replied firmly. "Just responsible. We're the ones who found it, Jake. That makes it our responsibility."

Jake shrugged, but there was no humour in his voice when he spoke again. "Yeah, I get it. I just... I don't want us to end up like her grandmother, hiding away some big secret and living in fear. If we're going to do this, we need to do it right."

Max shifted uncomfortably in his seat "I've been thinking about something," he said hesitantly. "The notebook isn't just about the wishes. It's about what it does to us. It feeds on our emotions—our doubts, our fears. Look at us right now. We're all on edge, arguing, second-guessing. Maybe breaking the cycle isn't just about a sacrifice. Maybe it's about proving that we're stronger than it."

The group fell silent, considering his words.

"That's a good point," Zara said after a moment. "If we let it control us, we've already lost. We need to stay focused, grounded. If we can't trust each other, we won't stand a chance."

A tentative plan began to take shape. They would need more than resolve; they would need clarity, unity, and a deeper understanding of the notebook's power.

"We'll take it slow," Ellie suggested. "No more impulsive decisions. We research everything we can—about the notebook, about sacrifices, about breaking curses. And we do it together."

"Agreed," Zara said, nodding. "But we also need to be prepared for the worst. If it comes down to making a sacrifice... we need to know what we're willing to give up."

The group exchanged uneasy glances, the weight of her words sinking in.

As the sun dipped below the horizon, casting the room in twilight, Ellie felt something shift within her. It wasn't a solution or a sense of certainty—just a faint glimmer of hope. For the first time in weeks, she didn't feel entirely alone in this fight.

228

Her grandmother's journal, now resting on the coffee table,

seemed less like a warning and more like a guide. The

sacrifices her grandmother had made, the pain she had

endured—it had all been for a purpose.

"We can do this," Ellie said, her voice barely above a whisper.

"We have to."

And for a moment, the storm clouds hanging over the group

seemed to part, revealing a path forward.

Chapter 16 – a Dangerous choice

The group gathered again the following weekend, this time at Ellie's house. The notebook, still encased in its box, sat in the centre of the table like an unwelcome guest. The weight of their last conversation lingered, and the air was thick with unease. Each of them knew they were running out of time to decide what to do.

"We can't avoid it forever," Zara said, breaking the silence. "We've talked about sacrifices, about breaking the cycle. But the question still stands: Are we willing to take the risk?"

Ellie glanced at the journal beside the box. Her grandmother's warnings echoed in her mind. The answer wasn't just about courage—it was about trust, unity, and resolve.

"I've been thinking," Ellie said hesitantly. "If we're going to use the notebook to resolve this, it can't be for something selfish. It must be for something bigger—something that justifies the cost."

"Bigger?" Jake interjected, his tone sceptical. "Like what? Ending world hunger? Fixing climate change? Those sound great, but have you thought about what that kind of wish might cost?"

"That's the problem," Theo added, arms crossed. "The notebook twists everything. Even if we wish for something good, the consequences could destroy everything we're trying to save."

Max fidgeted with his glasses, his nervous energy filling the room. "Maybe we don't have to use it at all," he suggested. "We could just lock it away again, try harder to secure it this time."

Ellie shook her head. "We've seen what happens when people try to hide it. It doesn't work. The notebook has a way of finding its way back into the world. If we don't do something permanent, it's only a matter of time before someone else finds it."

"So, what's the plan then?" Jake asked, leaning back in his chair. "We make some grand, noble wish and hope for the best?"

Zara, ever the pragmatist, leaned forward. "No. If we decide to use it, we need to be strategic. We need to think about every possible outcome, every potential consequence. This isn't a decision we can make lightly."

Ellie took a deep breath, her heart pounding. "I think we should wish to destroy the notebook," she said finally.

The room fell silent.

"Destroy it?" Max asked, his voice tinged with disbelief. "Can we even do that?"

"It's a risk," Ellie admitted. "But it's the only way to make sure no one else gets hurt. If we can figure out the right words, the right intention, we might be able to end this once and for all."

Theo frowned. "And what happens if the consequence of that wish is worse than anything we've seen so far? What if destroying the notebook unleashes whatever power it's been holding back?"

"We won't know unless we try," Ellie countered.

The group's debate grew heated, voices overlapping as they argued over the dangers and merits of Ellie's plan.

Jake was the first to speak against it. "This is insane. We don't even know if destroying the notebook is possible, let alone what it might cost. What if we're biting off more than we can chew?"

Max, ever cautious, nodded in agreement. "I'm with Jake. This feels... reckless."

Zara, however, sided with Ellie. "Sometimes the only way forward is through. If we keep avoiding the hard decisions, we're just delaying the inevitable."

Theo remained quiet, his expression unreadable. When he finally spoke, his voice was low but firm. "If we do this, we need to be ready for anything. No more half-measures. No more second-guessing."

After hours of discussion, the group finally reached a fragile consensus: they would attempt to use the notebook to destroy itself. But the details were still unclear.

"What if we phrase it wrong?" Max asked nervously. "What if we say the wrong thing and make everything worse?"

"That's why we'll plan it out," Zara assured him. "We'll take our time, write out exactly what we want to say, and think through every possible outcome."

Ellie nodded. "And we do it together. No one makes the wish alone."

As the group disbanded for the night, Ellie couldn't shake the feeling that something was wrong. The notebook seemed to hum with an almost imperceptible energy, as if it could sense their intentions.

She stared at the box long after the others had left, her mind racing with questions. Was this truly the right choice? Or were they walking into a trap they couldn't escape?

Ellie's grey tabby, Luna, hopped onto the table, nuzzling against her arm. The cat's presence was comforting, a small reminder of the normalcy she so desperately missed.

"We'll figure it out," Ellie whispered, more to herself than to Luna. "We have to."

But as she closed the journal and turned off the light, she couldn't shake the feeling that their choice, dangerous as it was, might not be theirs alone to make.

The following week, the group met again, this time at Zara's house. The notebook, still locked away in its wooden box, sat at the centre of their discussions. Despite their earlier consensus, tension filled the air as the gravity of their decision began to sink in.

Zara was the first to break the silence. "We've agreed to try destroying the notebook, but agreeing isn't the same as committing. If we go through with this, there's no turning back. We need to be absolutely certain."

Her words settled heavily over the group.

Ellie sat with her hands clasped tightly in her lap. "I'm certain," she said softly but firmly. "If we don't do this, the notebook will destroy someone else's life. Maybe someone who won't have the strength to fight back. We can't let that happen."

The others nodded, though some more hesitantly than others.

Jake sighed, running a hand through his hair. "Okay, but let's not pretend this is some noble, clean solution. Whatever price we're paying, it's going to be ugly. Are we really ready for that?"

"We have to be," Ellie replied, her gaze unwavering.

Zara stood, pacing the room as she spoke. "This isn't just about willingness. We need a plan. We need to decide exactly how we'll phrase the wish, and we need to prepare for whatever happens next. No improvising, no second-guessing. Once we start, we follow through."

Her words were practical, but there was an edge of vulnerability in her tone. She wasn't just trying to lead the group—she was trying to hold herself together.

"Agreed," Theo said, his voice unusually steady. "But we also need contingencies. If the wish goes sideways, we need to have a way to protect ourselves."

"How do you protect yourself from magic?" Max asked, his anxiety evident.

"By staying together," Zara replied. "No one faces this alone. That's non-negotiable."

As the group began brainstorming possible wish phrasing, each member wrestled with their own doubts and fears.

Ellie felt the weight of her grandmother's legacy. She couldn't help but wonder if she was strong enough to finish what her grandmother had started.

Zara struggled to keep her composure, the gnawing at her resolve.

Jake masked his unease with jokes, but his playful demeanour couldn't hide his growing fear.

Theo questioned every plan, not out of malice, but out of a deep-seated need to protect the group from potential disaster.

Max, ever the worrier, couldn't shake the feeling that they were missing something crucial.

By the end of the night, they had settled on a draft of the wish: "We wish for this notebook, and all its power, to cease to exist in all forms, leaving no trace behind."

They knew it wasn't perfect, but it was the best they could do.

"We have to stick together on this," Zara said, her voice resolute. "No matter what happens, no one backs out."

The group exchanged uneasy glances, but one by one, they nodded.

Jake, ever the joker, tried to lighten the mood. "Well, if this goes horribly wrong, at least we'll all go down in history. Or, you know, cease to exist with the notebook."

Despite themselves, a few of them chuckled.

Before they left, Ellie pulled out a small box she had brought with her. Inside were five matching bracelets, each made of simple braided threads.

"My grandmother used to say that symbols matter," Ellie explained. "They remind us of who we are and what we stand for. I thought... maybe these could remind us to stay strong. Together."

The group hesitated, then took the bracelets one by one, slipping them onto their wrists.

"Together," Zara said, her voice quiet but firm.

"Together," the others echoed.

As they left Zara's house that night, the group felt a fragile sense of unity. The path ahead was dangerous, but for the first time, they were committed to walking it together.

Ellie glanced down at her bracelet, the threads catching the light of the streetlamp. Her grandmother's words echoed in her mind: *"Symbols matter."*

She hoped they were enough.

Chapter 17 – The binding spell

The group gathered at Ellie's house this time, their nerves on edge as they prepared for what would likely be their most daring act yet. They sat in a circle on the living room floor, the notebook's wooden case resting in the centre like a sleeping beast. The tension in the room was palpable, each of them acutely aware that they were about to cross a line they could never return from.

"This isn't just about making a wish," Ellie said, breaking the silence. "We need to make sure the notebook can't twist it. We need safeguards."

Theo, who had spent the week researching protective rituals and spells in old books and obscure forums, nodded. "That's where the binding spell comes in. It won't stop the notebook from twisting the wish entirely, but it should at least limit its ability to manipulate us."

"Should?" Jake asked, raising an eyebrow. "Not exactly reassuring, man."

Theo shot him a withering look. "It's magic, not maths. There are no guarantees. But it's better than going in blind."

The group worked together to gather the materials Theo had listed:

- A circle of white chalk, drawn carefully on Ellie's hardwood floor.
- Five candles, one for each of them.
- A small mirror, symbolizing reflection and intent.
- A sprig of rosemary for protection, placed in the centre alongside the box.

Ellie's cat, Luna, watched from the corner, her eyes gleaming with an almost unnerving intelligence.

"Are we sure about this?" Max asked as he lit his candle. His hands trembled, but he managed to keep the flame steady.

"No," Zara said bluntly, lighting her own candle. "But we've made our choice. Now we follow through."

Theo stepped into the centre of the circle, holding the notebook's case in his hands. "The spell is about intent," he explained. "We each have to focus on the same goal: binding the notebook's power to our will, limiting its ability to harm us."

He set the box down and began to recite the incantation he had pieced together from various sources. His voice was steady, but the words carried an almost otherworldly weight.

The others joined hands, their eyes fixed on the notebook's case as Theo's chant filled the room. The candles flickered, their flames bending inward as if drawn toward the centre of the circle.

Ellie felt a strange warmth radiating through her bracelet, the threads seeming to hum with energy. She glanced at the others and saw the same resolve mirrored in their faces.

As Theo reached the final lines of the incantation, the room grew unnaturally still. The air felt heavy, as though it were pressing down on them. The candles' flames turned blue, casting eerie shadows on the walls.

And then, with a sharp crack, the box flew open.

The notebook lay inside, its pages fluttering as if caught in a phantom wind. A low, guttural whisper filled the room, a language none of them could understand.

"What's happening?" Max cried, his grip tightening on Zara's hand.

Theo's voice rose above the chaos. "Hold the circle! Don't let go!"

The group tightened their grip on one another, their shared determination forming an invisible barrier against the notebook's power. Ellie focused on the bracelet around her wrist, willing its symbolic strength to anchor her.

The whispering grew louder, more insistent, but the group held firm. Slowly, the notebook's pages began to still, the blue flames returning to their normal golden hue.

When the silence finally fell, it was deafening.

Theo knelt to close the box, his hands trembling. "It worked," he said, though he sounded more uncertain than triumphant. Ellie picked up the box, her fingers brushing its now-warm surface. "It feels... different," she said. "Like it's quieter somehow."

Zara nodded. "The binding spell might not have solved everything, but it's a start. At least now we have a fighting chance."

As the group cleaned up the remnants of the ritual, their relief was tempered by the knowledge that their journey was far from over.

"Do you think the notebook knows what we're planning?" Max asked quietly, his gaze darting toward the closed box.

"I think it always knows," Theo replied, his expression grim.

Ellie looked at her friends, their faces etched with exhaustion and resolve. For better or worse, they were bound to the notebook—and to each other.

The group met again later that week, the air was heavy with purpose as the group gathered in Ellie's living room. The notebook sat locked in its wooden case at the centre of the table, the faint hum of its power almost palpable. Each member of the group carried their own mix of fear, resolve, and uncertainty, but they had all agreed: it was time to end this.

As the group sat around the table, their draft of the carefully worded wish in front of them, Theo suddenly frowned. He had been flipping through a collection of notes they had gathered during their research—pages from Ellie's grandmother's journal, sketches of the notebook, and scraps of translated text from obscure tomes.

246

"Wait," Theo said, breaking the tense silence.

Everyone looked up at him.

"What is it?" Ellie asked.

Theo tapped a finger against one of the translated texts.

"We've been assuming the notebook's power only responds when we write something down, right?"

"Yeah, that's literally how it works," Jake said, shrugging. "We write, and it twists stuff. That's the whole problem."

"But" Theo continued, "what if it's more than that? Look at this." He pointed to a passage in the journal. "Ellie's grandmother wrote here about the notebook responding to intent, not just the act of writing. 'A thought becomes as dangerous as ink in its presence,' she said. What if... what if we don't need to write the wish at all? What if it already knows what we want?"

The group fell silent, processing Theo's revelation.

"Are you saying," Zara began slowly, "that the notebook is... listening to us? That it's aware of what we're thinking?"

Theo nodded. "It makes sense. Think about it—why else would the notebook twist wishes in such specific ways? It's not just interpreting the words we write, it's reacting to what we *mean*. And if that's true, then maybe we don't need to write the wish to destroy it. Maybe it just needs us to fully commit to the idea."

"That's insane," Max said, his voice rising. "You want us to sit here and *think* it into oblivion? What if we're wrong? What if it twists our thoughts just like it twists our words?"

"We've already seen signs of this," Ellie said softly, her mind flashing back to moments when the notebook seemed to respond to their unspoken emotions—the colours of its pages shifting, the subtle way it seemed to react to their fears.

Jake leaned back in his chair, his arms crossed. "So let me get this straight. We've been stressing over writing the perfect wish for days, and now you're saying we might not even need to write it?"

"Exactly," Theo replied. "But it must be unanimous. The notebook won't respond unless we're all on the same page, literally and figuratively. If even one of us hesitates, it won't work."

"Unanimous, huh?" Jake said, smirking. "No pressure or anything."

Zara cut in, her voice firm. "If this is true, then it's even more important that we're clear about our intent. No doubts, no second-guessing. We must want the same thing, with no hesitation."

The group spent the next hour discussing every angle of the decision. What would happen if they succeeded? What if they failed? Could they truly let go of the notebook, knowing what it was capable of?

Ellie took the lead, her calm, steady voice guiding them. "We've seen what it can do. The good and the bad. But keeping it means risking more harm—not just to us, but to anyone who might find it in the future. If we let it go now, we can stop that from happening. Together."

One by one, they agreed.

"I'm in," Zara said.

"Let's do it," Jake added, though his tone betrayed a trace of nervousness.

"I'm scared, but... yeah. Let's end this," Max said.

Theo nodded. "Let's try it."

"We've tested everything we could," Zara began, her voice steady but low. "The binding spell held during the last few days. No strange dreams, no whispers in the night. If there's ever a time to do this, it's now."

Ellie nodded, her fingers absently tracing the threads of her bracelet. "This is our chance. But we must get it right. No loopholes, no vague wording."

The group huddled around a piece of paper, scribbling down possible phrasings for their wish.

"We have to be direct," Theo said, his tone sharp with focus. "Something like, 'We wish for the notebook and all its power to be completely and permanently destroyed.'"

Jake frowned. "Yeah, but what if it twists that to mean something like... destroying us because we're tied to its power now?"

"That's why we need to add specifics," Ellie said, her brow furrowed. "We have to cover every angle."

They revised the phrasing over and over, adding layers of clarification:

"We wish for the notebook, along with all its magical properties, to cease to exist in any form, this wish must not harm any living being or cause unintended consequences, the wish must fulfil its purpose without affecting the wisher or their environment."

Despite their efforts, the lingering uncertainty gnawed at them.

As the group took a break, the weight of their task began to sink in.

"What if this doesn't work?" Max asked, his voice barely above a whisper. "What if it's just too powerful to destroy?"

Zara placed a reassuring hand on his shoulder. "If we don't try, we'll never know. And we can't just keep letting it exist, not after everything we've seen."

Jake leaned back against the couch, trying to mask his anxiety with humour. "Worst case scenario, we all get zapped into some alternate dimension. At least it'd be interesting."

Ellie managed a small smile at his joke, but her gaze remained fixed on the box. "We're doing the right thing," she said, more to herself than anyone else.

As night fell, they lit candles around the room, hoping the light would offer some measure of comfort. The notebook case sat in the centre of a protective circle, the same one they had used for the binding spell.

"We'll all take turns reading the wish," Zara said, holding the piece of paper. "That way, it's a shared effort. The notebook won't be able to single any one of us out."

Ellie's cat, Luna, jumped onto the table and curled up next to the case. Her presence was oddly calming, a reminder of the normalcy they were fighting to protect.

Before they began, Ellie spoke. "No matter what happens tonight, I want you all to know... I couldn't have done any of this without you. We've been through so much together, and I—" Her voice caught, and she looked down, embarrassed.

Zara stepped forward, placing a hand on Ellie's shoulder. "We're in this together. All of us. And we'll see it through."

One by one, they clasped hands, forming a circle around the notebook.

"Ready?" Zara asked, her voice steady but soft.

"Ready," they all echoed.

With trembling hands, Ellie opened the box. The notebook seemed to shimmer in the candlelight, its presence overwhelming yet strangely subdued.

Zara took a deep breath and began to read the wish aloud, her voice firm and deliberate. The others followed, each reciting the words with as much conviction as they could muster.

As the final word was spoken, the air in the room shifted. The candles flickered violently, and a low, resonant hum filled the space. The notebook's pages began to flutter, glowing faintly as if resisting their command.

Ellie tightened her grip on Zara's hand, her heart pounding in her chest.

The hum grew louder, a vibration that seemed to rattle the very walls. The group held firm, their collective will focused on the wish they had crafted together.

Suddenly, the glow from the notebook intensified, filling the room with blinding light. For a moment, it felt as though time itself had stopped.

And then, just as abruptly, the light vanished.

The group blinked, disoriented.

"Did it work?" Max whispered, his voice trembling.

"I think..." she began, her voice breaking. "I think it's over."

The living room was silent, save for the soft crackle of a candle on the table. For the first time since they'd discovered the notebook, the group felt an overwhelming sense of emptiness, as though a tether binding them to something immense had snapped.

Zara broke the silence, her voice barely above a whisper. "It's really over, isn't it?"

Ellie nodded, her gaze fixed on the empty spot where the notebook had been. "It is. We did it."

Jake let out a low whistle, leaning back in his chair. "I half-expected it to turn into a phoenix or something and fly off with a sinister laugh. You know, one last twist."

The others laughed nervously, but the humour didn't quite land. The weight of what they'd done—and what they'd lost—lingered.

For days after the notebook's destruction, life felt... off. There was no buzzing sense of possibility, no strange colours on the edges of their vision, no whispers in the night. The absence of the notebook's presence was stark, and it left a void they weren't sure how to fill.

Ellie found herself sketching more than usual, her drawings infused with themes of light and shadow. Luna curled beside her on the couch, purring softly, as if sensing her unease.

Zara buried herself in books and projects, trying to distract herself from the lingering "what-ifs." Could they have used the notebook to help someone in need, to make the world a better place?

Jake tried to shake the tension by cracking more jokes than usual, but even he felt the undercurrent of change. "It's weird not having something magical messing with our heads," he admitted one afternoon. "I mean, it's good. But... weird."

Max, who had been the most nervous about the notebook from the start, seemed the most relieved. "I don't miss it," he said during one of their gatherings. "Not one bit. I don't care how many wishes it could've granted—it wasn't worth the cost."

"But don't you think..." Zara hesitated, her fingers tracing the edge of her coffee cup. "Don't you think we could have done something good with it? If we'd just been more careful?"

Max shook his head firmly. "That's the trap, though. Thinking you can control something like that. We did the right thing."

Theo, usually the sceptic, had been unusually quiet since the notebook vanished. When Ellie asked him about it, he shrugged. "It's not that I miss it or anything. I just... wonder what it all meant. Why us? Why your grandmother? Why that notebook?"

Ellie didn't have an answer. The questions gnawed at her too, but she knew they might never find the answers.

"Maybe it's not about the notebook," she said finally. "Maybe it's about what we did. How we handled it."

Theo gave her a rare smile. "Yeah. Maybe."

As the weeks passed, the group found their way back to normalcy—or something close to it. Ellie, Zara, Max, Theo, and Jake had been through something extraordinary, something few others could understand. And though the notebook was gone, the experience had left its mark on them all.

They had learned to trust each other, to confront their fears, and to let go of something they could never truly control.

One evening, Ellie sat on her bed, Luna nestled in her lap. She stared at her sketchpad, flipping through pages filled with images of the notebook, the group, and the strange journey they'd shared.

As she reached the last blank page, she picked up her pencil and began to draw.

Not the notebook, not the box, but the five of them sitting in a circle, hands clasped, united by their shared resolve.

When she finished, she smiled faintly.

Letting go didn't mean forgetting. It meant moving forward.

Chapter 18 – The new beginning

The seasons had begun to shift, bringing with them a crispness in the air that hinted at change. For the first time in months, the group found themselves not bound by the weight of the notebook, but instead meeting purely for the sake of reconnecting. They gathered at Ellie's house, her cozy living room a comforting backdrop for their shared stories, laughter, and plans for the future.

Ellie's grey tabby, Luna, was perched on the windowsill, observing the group with her usual quiet curiosity. The cat had become something of a symbol for their shared journey— steadfast, watchful, and a reminder of the little things that grounded them in reality.

"So, what now?" Jake asked, leaning back into Ellie's plush armchair with his typical carefree grin. "No more magical notebooks. No more life-altering decisions. What are we supposed to do with all this free time?"

"Maybe we live," Zara said simply, her voice calm but purposeful. "We've spent so much time thinking about what could happen, what might go wrong... maybe it's time to focus on what's right in front of us."

Max nodded, adjusting his glasses. "Honestly, I've been looking forward to boring. No more cryptic messages or crazy consequences. Just... normal life for a while."

Theo smirked, his sarcasm intact despite their recent growth. "Define 'normal.'"

Ellie laughed softly, her auburn hair catching the light as she turned to look at her friends. "Maybe normal isn't so bad. Maybe it's exactly what we need right now."

Each of them had been changed by their experience with the notebook, and now, with its absence, they were starting to see how those changes could shape their lives.

Ellie, once content to observe from the sidelines, had grown into a quiet but capable leader. She found herself taking more initiative, not just within the group but in her personal life, too. Zara had learned to let go of perfection, realizing that it wasn't about having all the answers but about trusting those around her.

Max was slowly shedding his anxieties, finding courage in the knowledge that he had faced one of the most daunting challenges imaginable and come out stronger.

Theo, the loner, was discovering the value of connection. He still preferred solitude at times, but he no longer viewed his friends as a burden.

Jake, the wildcard, had begun to temper his impulsiveness with a newfound sense of responsibility, without losing the spark of creativity and humour that defined him.

Their conversations that evening drifted between light-hearted banter and deeper reflection. Memories of their time with the notebook surfaced now and then, but they were shared without the weight of regret or fear.

"I think," Ellie said thoughtfully, "that everything happened for a reason. The notebook, my grandmother's journal, all of it… it brought us together in a way nothing else could have."

Zara smiled. "And now, we move forward. Together."

"Even if Jake's jokes drive us insane," Theo added, earning a chorus of laughter.

As the night wore on, the group began to share their hopes for the future. Zara spoke of her plans to start a new project, Ellie mentioned an art exhibition she was working toward, and Max shyly admitted he was thinking of joining a debating club.

When it was Jake's turn, he leaned forward dramatically. "I'm thinking… stand-up comedy. Thoughts?"

"Thoughts?" Theo deadpanned. "Yes. Don't."

The room erupted in laughter, the kind that came easily between friends who had been through everything together.

As the group finally dispersed for the night, Ellie lingered at the door, watching them leave one by one. When the last goodbye was said, she turned back to Luna, who was now curled up on the couch.

"This is it, girl," she whispered, scratching behind Luna's ears. "A fresh start."

And as she turned off the lights and climbed the stairs to her room, she felt a quiet sense of peace. The notebook was gone, but what it had taught them—and the bond it had forged—would remain.

It started subtly, small moments that passed without much notice until they began to connect in unexpected ways. The group's bond had always been strong, but in the absence of the notebook's turmoil, something deeper began to emerge.

Ellie sat in her favourite café, sketchpad in hand. Her drawings had taken on a softer tone lately—portraits of her friends mingled with abstract shapes that hinted at emotions she couldn't quite name.

Her pencil hovered over the page as her thoughts drifted to Theo. His sharp wit and guarded demeanour had always intrigued her, but now she found herself noticing the moments in between—the quiet glances, the way he softened when he spoke to her.

It wasn't something she'd planned or expected, but it was there, undeniable.

Across town, Zara and Jake were walking through the park, the autumn leaves crunching underfoot. Jake was cracking jokes, as always, but Zara noticed something different in his tone—an earnestness that hadn't been there before.

"Do you ever take anything seriously?" she teased, nudging him with her shoulder.

Jake smirked. "Oh, I take plenty seriously. You, for example."

She paused, caught off guard. "Me?"

"Yeah," he said, shrugging casually. "You're always the one holding everything together. Someone's got to make sure you don't forget to let loose every now and then."

Zara laughed, but her heart skipped a beat. Was it just Jake being Jake, or was there more to his words than she'd realised?

Meanwhile, Max found himself spending more time with Ellie, helping her organise her art supplies or just keeping her company while she sketched.

He admired her creativity and her ability to see the world in ways he couldn't. There was something calming about being around her, like she had a way of grounding him when his thoughts spiralled.

But he also felt a pang of uncertainty. Did she see him the same way, or was he just the reliable friend she leaned on?

Theo wasn't blind to the shifting dynamics. He'd always prided himself on being the one to notice what others missed, and lately, he'd seen the way Ellie's eyes lingered on him a moment longer than usual.

It scared him. Opening up had never come easily, and the idea of letting someone in that close felt like walking into uncharted territory.

But when she smiled at him, or when her sketches captured something about him he didn't even realise he'd shown, he felt something he couldn't ignore—a warmth, a pull, a possibility.

None of them were ready to talk about it outright, but something was there, woven into their interactions, shaping the way they saw one another and themselves.

At their next gathering, the group felt the unspoken shift.

There was more laughter, more lingering glances, more

moments that felt charged with meaning.

For now, they didn't need to define it. They had time to figure

out what these feelings meant and what to do with them.

Epilogue

The hum of the airplane engines was a steady backdrop as Ellie stared out the window, watching the clouds drift far below. The world stretched vast beneath them, a reminder of just how small their town—and their problems—had once seemed. She glanced over at her friends, all seated nearby, each absorbed in their own thoughts. It had been months since they last touched the notebook, and yet, its presence still lingered in their lives, not as an object of fear, but as a lesson they had all learned together.

Zara sat upright, flipping through the pages of a travel guide, ever the planner. Next to her, Max had his headphones in, nodding slightly to a rhythm only he could hear. Theo, half-asleep, rested his head against the window, and Jake, of course, was playing some kind of guessing game with the flight attendant, his energy never quite dimming.

Ellie sighed, stretching her arms. "It still feels weird, doesn't it? Being able to just... move forward?"

Zara looked up from her book. "Yeah. But good weird. We needed this."

The trip had been planned months ago, even before everything with the notebook had spiralled into chaos. It had started as a joke—"Let's just run away for a bit"—but the more they talked about it, the more real it became. Now, here they were, flying halfway across the world for an adventure with no supernatural strings attached.

For the first time in what felt like forever, the future was their own.

It wasn't easy letting go. For weeks after they had decided to move on, Ellie had felt the weight of the notebook pressing on the edges of her mind. Would it find its way back to them? Had they really broken free? But as the days passed, the intensity of those thoughts faded. Life returned to normal, or at least as normal as it could be after everything they had been through.

Theo had been the first to say it out loud. "Maybe it was never about the magic. Maybe it was always about what we thought we wanted."

Max had agreed, and even Jake, ever the wildcard, had admitted that he was relieved to leave it behind.

They had grown—whether they realised it or not. Ellie could see it in the way Zara didn't rush to take charge of every decision anymore, in the way Max seemed more confident, in the way Theo allowed himself to trust them, and in how Jake, despite his joking, had learned when to take things seriously. And Ellie? She had found her own voice, not just as an observer, but as a leader.

The flight attendant came by, offering drinks. Ellie took a juice and smiled when Jake tried to barter for an extra snack. Some things never changed.

"So," Theo murmured, stretching as he finally woke up.

"What's the plan once we land?"

Zara tapped her book. "We check into the hostel, grab some food, and then explore the city. No rigid schedules, just vibes."

"Did you just say, 'just vibes'?" Max raised an eyebrow. "I never thought I'd see the day."

"Shut up," Zara muttered, but there was a smile on her face.

Jake leaned forward. "I vote we find the weirdest tourist attraction and start there. Something haunted."

Theo groaned. "Why do you always want ghosts?"

Ellie laughed, the sound light and free. "Fine, fine. No ghosts. Just... whatever we want."

And that was the truth of it, wasn't it? For so long, their choices had felt dictated by something beyond them—the notebook, the consequences, the weight of their own desires. But not anymore. This trip, this moment, was something they had built together, and no magic was pulling the strings.

The hum of the engines continued, a steady vibration that mixed with the muffled voices of passengers and the occasional ding of the overhead announcements. Outside, clouds stretched endlessly, golden at the edges from the setting sun.

It had been hours since take-off, and boredom was setting in. Ellie, sketchbook open on her tray table, glanced at the others.

"Alright, I have a question."

Jake perked up instantly. "Ooooh, I love a good question."

She smirked. "Do you guys think we actually have *free will*?"

Max, who had been flipping through an in-flight magazine, groaned. "Oh no. This is going to be *one of those* discussions, isn't it?"

Theo, arms crossed, raised an eyebrow. "You don't think it's an interesting question?"

"I think it's a question that has no real answer," Max countered. "Which means we'll end up going in circles until Jake says something ridiculous."

Jake gasped dramatically. *"How dare you?* I take philosophical discussions *very* seriously."

Zara rolled her eyes. "Alright, fine. Free will. Let's go. What's your take, Ellie?"

Ellie tapped her pencil against the sketchpad. "I don't know. Sometimes I think we're making choices, but other times... it feels like everything's already *set*, like we're just following a path we don't even realise was laid out for us."

Theo nodded. "Like fate."

Jake pointed at him. "Or like a *glitch in the simulation*."

Max sighed. "Here we go."

"No, hear me out," Jake said, sitting up. "What if we *think* we have free will, but we're just running on some kind of pre-coded system? Every choice we make feels real, but it's just the illusion of choice."

Zara smirked. "So, we're *NPCs* in some cosmic video game?"

Jake nodded seriously. "Exactly."

Max rubbed his temples. "That doesn't even make sense. If we were programmed, we wouldn't *feel* like we had choices at all."

"But what if the programming is *so good* that we *can't* tell?" Jake shot back.

Theo leaned in, intrigued. "Okay, but what if it's both? What if we have choices, but only within a certain framework? Like, we can pick our paths, but the world around us still has limits."

Ellie considered that. "Like a giant choose-your-own-adventure book?"

Zara snapped her fingers. "Exactly. We don't control *everything*, but we still shape our own outcomes."

Jake sighed dramatically. "So, we're *not* in a simulation?"

Max shook his head. "No, Jake. We're not in a simulation."

Jake slumped back in his seat. "Fine. But if we *were*, I'd totally want to hack the system."

Theo smirked. "Of course you would."

They sat in thoughtful silence for a moment, the steady hum of the plane filling the gaps between their words.

Ellie glanced out the window, watching the clouds drift by.

Maybe they'd never know the *real* answer. Maybe free will was just another question with a thousand possible answers.

But maybe that was okay.

Because whether they were following a path or making their own, one thing was for sure—right now, they were exactly where they were supposed to be.

The plane hummed beneath them, a steady rhythm that seemed to carry their thoughts forward. The conversation had started with a simple question—*do we have free will?* —but now it was evolving into something deeper.

Ellie leaned back in her seat, staring at the ceiling as she spoke. "Okay, so let's say we *do* have choices... but every choice we make is already influenced by something else. And those influences are influenced by things before them. Doesn't that mean our choices are *never* truly free?"

Zara tapped a finger against her armrest. "You're talking about determinism—the idea that everything that happens is caused by something before it."

Theo nodded. "Right. Like, you didn't just decide to ask that question randomly. Something made you think of it. Maybe it was something you read. Or something we said earlier. Either way, you didn't pull it from nowhere."

Max adjusted his glasses. "And if that's true, then every choice we make is really just the *only* choice we *could* have made, based on everything that's come before it."

Jake frowned. "So, you're saying we're *stuck*? That we don't get to decide anything?"

Ellie shrugged. "Not *stuck*, exactly. Just... limited. Like, every moment is shaped by the ones before it. We exist in a framework—of past decisions, of past events, of physical laws. We can make choices, but only within that framework."

Jake scoffed. "That sounds like being stuck."

Theo smirked. "Depends on how you look at it. Maybe we're not stuck. Maybe we're just *riding the wave* of everything that's already happened."

Zara folded her arms. "But if everything is interconnected— every choice leading to another, every event shaping the next—then in a way, we're just following a script we can't see."

Jake groaned. "This is depressing."

Ellie smiled. "Not necessarily. Just because we're influenced by the past doesn't mean our choices don't matter. We *do* make decisions, even if they're limited by everything that came before. And those decisions create new events, which shape future choices. It's all connected."

Max rubbed his chin. "So... we don't have absolute free will, but we do have *some* control?"

Theo shrugged. "More like... we have control within limits. We can move, but only within the boundaries of what already exists."

Jake leaned forward. "Okay, but what if we *break* the framework? What if we make a choice so random, so completely unexpected, that it throws everything off?"

Zara rolled her eyes. "And what, exactly, would that look like?"

Jake grinned, unbuckled his seatbelt, and stood up. "I could scream right now. Just—shout something ridiculous. Everyone would freak out. It would change the course of this flight. New variables, new outcomes. *Boom.* Framework broken."

Max pulled him back into his seat. "Or, you know, *security would get involved* and your choice would still have predictable consequences."

Jake sighed. "Fine. So, I'm still part of the system."

Theo smirked. "Welcome to reality."

They all sat there for a moment, letting it sink in. Maybe they weren't *completely* free. Maybe every choice was shaped by a thousand invisible threads, pulling them in directions they didn't even realise.

But they *could* still move.

Even if they were in a web, they could choose which thread to follow.

The plane continued to hum predictably accompanied by the quiet conversations of passengers and the occasional rustle of snack wrappers. The group had already tackled free will and the limits of choice, but Ellie wasn't done thinking yet. She turned her pencil over in her fingers and glanced at the others. "Okay, new question. Where do new ideas come from?"

Jake groaned. "Ellie, I was just about to take a nap."

Zara smirked. "Too bad. Now I'm interested."

Theo stretched in his seat. "Depends on what you mean by 'new.' Do you mean ideas that have *never* existed before, or just ideas that are *new to us*?"

Ellie considered that. "Well... both, I guess."

Max adjusted his glasses. "I don't think anything comes from *nowhere*. Every idea is built on something else. Even when we think we're being creative, we're really just remixing things we've already seen, heard, or experienced."

Theo nodded. "Yeah, it's like—imagine a painter. They might create something *new*, but every brushstroke is influenced by colours they've seen before, techniques they've studied, emotions they've felt. Their art didn't appear out of thin air."

Zara tapped her chin. "So, originality is just *rearranging* things in a way no one has done before?"

Jake, now intrigued, sat up. "Wait, wait, wait—what about dreams? I've had some *wild* dreams that didn't come from anywhere. I once dreamed that Milo was a time traveller who got stuck in ancient Rome. That's got to be original."

Max sighed. "Even that isn't totally random. Your brain pulls from things you already know—history, time travel stories, your pet. Dreams just mix them in ways you wouldn't think of when you're awake."

Ellie nodded. "So, ideas come from *connections*—taking different things we already know and combining them into something new?"

Theo smirked. "Pretty much. It's like a puzzle. Every idea is just pieces of other ideas put together in a way no one else has tried yet."

Jake's eyes lit up. "So *that's* why I'm a genius. I just connect things in ways normal people don't."

Zara snorted. "Yeah, sure. That's *exactly* it."

They sat with the thought for a moment.

Ideas weren't born out of nothing. They came from the world, from experiences, from knowledge passed down through time. Every invention, every piece of art, every joke, every song—it all came from something *before*.

And yet, somehow, there was still room for *newness*.

Ellie glanced down at her sketchbook, at the unfinished lines of a drawing she hadn't planned yet.

Maybe the real magic wasn't in creating something out of nothing.

Maybe it was in taking what already *existed* and finding a way to make it *feel* brand new.